HELP
I'M
GETTING
MARRIED
TOMORROW!

Books in the Series

Help! I'm Getting Married Tomorrow
10 Things We Wish the Church Would Teach Brides-to-Be about Sex
Spring 2022

Book One of The Good*Christian Sex Guide Series

HELP I'M GETTING MARRIED TOMORROW!

10 Things We Wish the Church Would Teach
Brides-to-Be about Sex

**Dr. David Olamide Craig &
Aisha Nkiru Craig**

Published in England, United Kingdom by the Craig Christian Center.

Unless otherwise noted, scripture quotations are from the Holy Bible, *New Living Translation*, copyright 1996. Used by permission of Tyndale House Publishers, Inc., Wheaton, Illinois 60189. All rights reserved.
For all other versions quoted, see reverse.

A CIP catalogue record for this book is available from the British Library.

Paperback ISBN 978-1-7398928-0-7 / Ebook ISBN 978-1-7398928-1-4

Editor: Christina Roth. Illustrations: El Mehdi Najdi.
Typesetting: Craig Christian Center. Cover design: Olamide Craig

Disclaimer: This book contains advice and information relating to sexual health and emotional well-being. It is not intended to replace medical or psychotherapeutic advice and should not be used to replace regular care by your doctor or mental health professional.

While all efforts have been made to ensure the accuracy of the information contained in this book as of the date of publication, this information may be subject to change.

Parts of this book reflect the authors' present recollections of client consultations and experiences over time. All client names and characteristics have been changed to protect their identity, some stories have been coalesced, some events have been compressed and some dialogue has been recreated.

Warning: This book contains adult content and potentially triggering themes.

For our daughter,

Catherine Ayomide Chidinma Amina Craig

To our mothers,

Kehinde TemilolaOluwa Craig and Obianuju Jemila Yusuf.

Thank you for teaching us the way of the Lord.

CONTENTS

FOREWORD

As a certified marriage coach and relationship counsellor with over twenty years of experience, I know that a lack of sexual intimacy and sexual satisfaction can have serious consequences in any marriage. Christian marriages are not exempt from this, and in fact, it would appear that they are sometimes disproportionately affected by it.

But how do we hope to address this when we don't talk about sex in the church? This book is set to change that.

I have known Dr. Craig for many years, and he and his wife, Aisha, are passionate about helping Christian couples navigate sex and sexuality the way God intended. It is no wonder that they have put together such an informative and well-written book.

In the chapters ahead, Olamide and Aisha take us on a journey through scripture, cross-referencing Bible passages to reveal true biblical sexuality while boldly confronting centuries of misinformation. This field manual for brides-to-be provides all the basic information they need to know about sex before they get married.

The Craigs invite us to learn from the experiences of their clients and share the deep knowledge and expertise gained in their Christian sexuality counselling practice. They combine this with peer-reviewed studies to produce a well-rounded and thoroughly researched book that is sure to be a blessing to the church.

Ultimately, this book is a must-read for Christian women who will have no prior sexual experience on their wedding night, but married couples will find it invaluable too, especially if they have not been enjoying the full benefits of sexual intimacy in marriage. It is full of practical wisdom and applicable information that is not only scripture based but also medically proven, and will teach brides and brides-to-be how to not neglect their own sexual needs while meeting the sexual needs of their husbands.

I highly recommend the Craigs and this book as a resource to resolve both the unsaid and unmet expectations in the 'other room'.

Kingsley Okonkwo
Senior Pastor, David's Christian Centre
Founder, Love, Dating and Marriage Ministries

ABOUT THIS BOOK

One day in 2016, Dr. Craig got a direct message on Instagram from a young lady. Her question went something like this:

Rev. Dr. Craig, please, I need your help. I and my husband-to-be have decided to save sex for marriage, and we are both virgins. Could you give us some advice on how to have sex for the first time? Does it have to be painful? Am I going to bleed? I don't want my first experience to be terrible.

As relationship counsellors and leaders in church ministry, we help Christians handle marital issues from a godly perspective. Often, these issues involve the spiritual, emotional, psychological and physical aspects of sex. As a physician, Dr. Craig has a unique perspective on the anatomical aspects of sex.

We both read the young lady's message and prayerfully responded by email with what evolved into the first draft of this book.

Over the years we have sent out different versions of that email to our friends and family who were soon getting married. Today that email has morphed into a book series, written specifically for Christian believers who have honoured God by saving sex for marriage. We believe that honouring God should not have to put any Christian couple at a disadvantage when it comes to sexual information and education, and our desire is to equip the saints so that they lack no good thing (Ephesians 4:12, Psalm 34:10).

This book is intended for *engaged* women who are *at least* three months to their wedding. We designed this book (and its companion title for men) to be used by intending couples as part of their premarital classes in churches. We hope that it will be purchased by couples before their wedding or presented to them as gifts by peers, Christian mentors, parents or clergy as a way to support wholesome Christian sexuality.

We have intentionally kept the language simple, approaching each concept from a beginner's perspective in an easy-to-read, Bible-based and science-backed format. For further study and deeper insight, we have included our references and commentary in the footnotes.

Each chapter of this book represents one of ten crucial topics we believe the church should be teaching brides-to-be about sex. The chapters are ordered as a suggestion, but you are welcome to read them in the order that best meets your immediate needs. (PS: Chapters 8 and 9 contain step-by-step instructions if your wedding really *is* tomorrow. Quick, what are you waiting for—we wrote this book just for you!)

We pray that the contents of these pages bless, edify and educate you, and we eagerly look forward to hearing all your testimonies.

His love—and ours,

Olamide and Aisha Craig

www.olamidecraig.com
@olamideandaisha

INTRODUCTION: THERE ARE NO FIRST-TIME EXPERTS

One of our all-time favourite athletes is the sensational Serena Williams. Almost everyone who has seen her play would agree that her talent is exceptional and her skill undeniable. She is a master of the craft and has won more Grand Slam titles than any other female tennis player alive.

We recently watched some of her old tennis matches, and as the footage rolled, it was easy to see how she had gotten more and more formidable with each tournament that she played. We could not help but notice the dedication and commitment she showed in practice, continually striving to improve her game. Serena truly embodies what is possible when a person chooses to invest time in developing a skill.

The world we live in today, with its high-speed Internet and the instant availability of social media content, combined with the infinite ability to airbrush, manipulate and curate an online persona, has led many people to believe in the fallacy of the 'overnight success'. However, as anyone who has ever been successful at anything will tell you, there is no such thing as an overnight success! Behind every victory, celebration and recognition are thousands of hours of hard work and dedication. In the real world, outside the social media facade, no one becomes the GOAT (greatest of all time) without putting in the work. **Champions may be crowned in the ring, but they are made in the gym.**

The same is true about sex. No one is born an Adonis or an Aphrodite. No one comes out of the womb with all the skills required to be good in bed or to be a good lover. In fact, most people will tell you that their first time left them mostly dissatisfied. And that is totally fine. Who could imagine today that the great Serena Williams was once an amateur player, giving away points and losing games?

Everyone starts somewhere, and your very first time at something is guaranteed to be not as good as your hundredth. And no matter how good or bad your first time is, it gets better the more time you have to practice and improve! There are no first-time experts. **You don't have to be a master at something you have never done before.**

Phew! Doesn't that take a huge load off your shoulders? It sure did ours when we got married, because neither of us had a lot of experience. When we said our vows in 2014, we entered our marriage as naive amateurs who were excited to grow and learn together.

Like most people reading this, you might have no sexual experience whatsoever. That's no problem. You are right where you need to be. We wrote this book mainly for you.

Maybe you have had sex before. Perhaps once or twice, or perhaps with someone you were in a long-term relationship with, or maybe it was a short-term fling or a one-night thing. We also wrote this book for you. We know too well the brokenness that results when sex is not done God's way, but we have also experienced first-hand the grace and forgiveness that is available when you trust God with your heart and rely on Him to heal and renew you.

Perhaps your previous sexual experience was with someone who had sex with you without your consent. Our heart goes out to you. We wrote this book for you too. When we were courting, Dr. Craig shared how during his childhood and adolescence he was sexually abused by people who were supposed to be trustworthy protectors, and how through the actions of others his innocence was stolen. This led to many years of pain, brokenness and confusion, and he ended up looking for love and completeness in a string of relationships, some of which ended up becoming sexual. It took several years, but he was able to find complete healing through Jesus, and from the ashes of his brokenness grew a ministry of sexual reconciliation spanning almost twenty years.

If you have been sexually active before, regardless of the circumstances, and you are getting married soon, be comforted in the truth that there is healing available at the cross. If you have not already done so, allow yourself to receive the healing and forgiveness that Christ died to purchase for you on the cross, over two thousand years ago. The Bible tells us that Christ atoned for every transgression, including the ones you have done and the ones done to you. He was wounded, and you were healed!

> But he was pierced for our transgressions; he was
> crushed for our iniquities; upon him was the
> chastisement that brought us peace, and with his
> wounds we are healed.
>
> Isaiah 53:5, ESV

Allow His peace to wash over you, and break every chain that may have formed between you and any previous partners. Emerge free from old covenants and enter boldly into your new season! You are healed and you are free! In Jesus's name! Amen.

There are no first-time experts. You don't have to be a master at something you have never done before.

The beautiful thing about married sex is that it is a first for everyone. The first time you have sex after your wedding is the first time you will be making love as husband and wife. We want you to approach sex with your husband like you would a new opportunity, to learn new things and unlearn old habits.

So go ahead, take a deep breath and relax. There is no pressure here. Our advice is for soon-to-be brides of all skill levels and everyone willing to learn. While we know that your first time may not be fireworks and fanfare, we believe that after reading this book, it will be a little less awkward, and you will have a lot more practical knowledge for building your sex life from zero to hero.

Are you ready? Let's go!

Prayer:

Dear Lord, thank You for this journey of learning and exploration. Help me to open my heart to You as I prepare for this new phase of my life with my husband. In Jesus's name, amen!

1

God Loves Sex

The Bible is brimming with sexual references, but if you look only on the surface, most of what you will find are warnings to avoid promiscuity, fornication and adultery. This is all well and good. However, if you look closely, you will find many passages that celebrate the beauty of sex in marriage.

In the book of Proverbs, the writer describes how a husband should derive pleasure from his wife's breasts, encouraging him to find satisfaction in them always:

> Rejoice in the wife of your youth.
> She is a loving deer, a graceful doe.
> Let her breasts satisfy you always.
>
> Proverbs 5:18b–19

Paul in his letter to the Corinthians encourages married couples to have sex regularly, and advises them not to *refuse* each other:

> So don't refuse sex to each other, unless you agree not to have sex for a little while, in order to spend time in prayer.
>
> 1 Corinthians 7:5, CEV

Sex is not a sin.
Fornication is.

And most racy of all is the Old Testament book Song of Songs (sometimes called the Songs of Solomon), a sensual celebration of love and eroticism between a betrothed and her beloved.

> I am weak from passion.
> His left hand is under my head,
> and his right hand caresses me.
>
> Song of Songs 2:5–6, GNT

The Song of Songs introduces us to a young woman and her husband-to-be. We meet them in the fields, playing hide-and-seek between the livestock, and as the story unfolds, we are taken on an extraordinary journey of longing and passion between two people who are clearly in love but are committed to keeping their relationship untainted by sexual sin. The writer explores this thoroughly, depicting scenes of great intensity followed by deep passion, close calls and near misses, then finishes with an instruction not to 'awaken love until it pleases' (Songs 8:4).

The Song of Songs also introduces us to an exciting new concept that we have termed *joyful anticipation*, which we explore in detail in Chapter 7. Throughout the book our lovers are depicted as thinking ahead about the joy that they would finally be able to experience when they consummate their love as husband and wife. To celebrate this, they compose erotic poetry and revel in the beauty and excitement of their bodies, albeit from a distance, and look forward to the passion they would one day be able to righteously share. You don't need to look too far to sense the sexual tension between our two lovers, and the scripture describes it in glorious detail.

She longs for him to kiss her:

> If only he would give me some of his kisses ...
> Oh, your loving is sweeter than wine!
>
> Song of Songs 1:2, CEB

But then she suggests that all their kisses are stolen in private and that she dare not kiss him in public, at least not without consequence. In fact, she wants to kiss him so much that she wishes he was her brother:

> Oh, I wish you were my brother,
> who nursed at my mother's breasts.
> Then I could kiss you no matter who was watching,
> and no one would criticize me.
>
> Song of Songs 8:1

When he comes to her door one night, she refuses to let him in:

> I slept, but my heart was awake,
> when I heard my lover knocking and calling:
> 'Open to me, my treasure, my darling,
> my dove, my perfect one ...'
> But I responded,
> 'I have taken off my robe.
> Should I get dressed again?
> I have washed my feet.
> Should I get them soiled?'
>
> Song of Songs 5:2–3

His desire for her is so strong that he tries to unbolt the gate but finds it locked. Eventually he decides against coming in, but by this time she describes herself as dripping with desire.

She changes her mind and decides to let him in, but by the time she goes to open the door for him, he is gone:

> My lover tried to unlatch the door,
> and my heart thrilled within me.
> I jumped up to open the door for my love,
> and my hands dripped with perfume.
> My fingers dripped with lovely myrrh
> as I pulled back the bolt.
> I opened to my lover,
> but he was gone!
>
> Song of Songs 5:4–6b

Some Bible scholars see an even deeper, more erotic meaning to this portion of the story, interpreting it to depict a time when the couple almost gave in to their passion, and were able to hold on, but just barely.[1]

However *you* choose to interpret it, the pattern of *joyful anticipation* is repeated throughout the eight chapters of this most sacred book of the Bible. We are taken along on their journey of erotic tension, deep longing and heartfelt devotion to each other, and as we walk alongside them, we are meant to see two important things:

First, we observe that the love between a man and a woman, and the erotic tension they share, is holy; holy enough that a no-holds-barred description of this kind of love made it into the Holy Bible.

Second, we are to understand that God desires to love us with the same intensity, and that the purpose of our lives is to seek Him with the same passion and devotion.

This concept of holy sexual tension may seem odd to modern conservative Christian readers, even though almost anyone who has ever been in love can relate to the feelings that our lovers describe. Nevertheless, the traditional position of very conservative churches (or at least the perception conveyed) has been that those feelings are sinful and should be avoided at all costs. We have counselled several engaged couples who struggled with guilt over even the most innocent of desires because they had grown up believing that, like sex, all romantic desire outside marriage is sin.

But **Sex is not a sin. Fornication is.**

Because for the most part, the complete biblical perspective on sex and sexuality is not taught in our churches, many conservative Christians have come to view the book of Song of Songs as an antithesis. They think of it almost as though it was misfiled, the way one would look at a chapter on quantum physics within a book of economics and fiscal policy. In a bid to reconcile this cognitive dissonance, the story is labelled an allegory, a parable describing the love God has for His people. Many conservative Christians cannot see any way for it to be anything else. There is no way that our holy God would be pleased with this kind of sensual and erotic love, right? Wrong! While the Song of Songs does indeed reflect God's love for His people, it is much more. So much more!

God is not ashamed of sex. He does not hide His face away when a married man and his wife make love. Quite the opposite. We believe that He is right there in the midst of them, blessing their pleasure and receiving their praise.

Rabbi Adam Greenwald in his article 'Kisses Sweeter Than Wine' has this to say about the Song of Songs:

> It is unsurprising, given the racy nature of the Song of Songs, that its inclusion in the biblical canon was a matter of some controversy. In fact, it seems that it would have been excluded from the Bible altogether,

if it did not have a powerful champion: As the Sages debated which books were to be included in the Scriptures, it is said that Rabbi Akiva—certainly the greatest rabbi of his era (late first century, early second century)—weighed in that 'while all of the sacred writings are holy, the Song of Songs is the holy of holies!'

(Mishnah, Yadayim 3:5).[2]

Sexual intimacy helps bring couples closer and builds a bond that would be very difficult to forge otherwise. There is something to be said of the complete union that occurs when two bodies and two souls are joined together in lovemaking, and how for even just a moment, we lose all inhibitions and limitations; how we cease to be two distinct people, but meld into one entity of vibrant pulsations, how the thrusting of our hips echoes the rhythms of our pounding hearts, and the duet of our voices calls out His name as we approach the height of ecstasy.

The Bible is very clear about sex:

Sex is good.
Sex is holy.
Sex should be between husband and wife.
Sex builds intimacy.
Sex is for procreation.
Sex gives us pleasure.
Sex gives God glory.

The Bible never tells us that sex is sinful, or evil, or wrong. Instead of telling our children and young adults that sex equals sin, we believe that the church should be telling them that **sex is righteous but reserved**. Reserved for a *specific person* (husband and wife) and for a *specific time* (after marriage).

As you embark on this journey of unlearning and discovery, we want you to be confident in the truth that God designed sex to be enjoyed in marriage, and we pray that this frees you to rejoice in what God has set ahead for you, with joyful anticipation and gladness!

Prayer

Dear Lord, thank You for showing me sex is righteous, and that the love between a man and his wife is holy. Help me to seek You with the same passion and devotion. In Jesus's name, amen!

Notes

1. *Poetic Interpretation:* In verse 2 the woman dreams that her fiancé calls out to her, and tells her of his desire to know her intimately. In verse 3 she declines, and tells him why she can't have sex with him, but in verse 4, consumed with desire, he reaches his hand towards her "gate" and attempts to unlock it. This arouses her feelings for him (Songs 5:4 NASB), so that in verse 5, she decides to open the gate and let her beloved in. By this time however, he has come to his senses, realises what must be done, (1 Corinthians 6:18) and in verse 6, he flees the scene. In this interpretation, our lovers avoid sin, but only just.

Does this sound familiar to you? Have you and your husband-to-be ever had a similar close shave?

2. Greenwald, Adam, 'Kisses Sweeter Than Wine: Understanding the Song of Songs', *My Jewish Learning*, https://www.myjewishlearning.com/article/song-of-songs/, accessed 10 Jul. 2021.

The idea that the Song of Songs is too raunchy to be in the Bible is as old as the Bible itself, but we are reminded that this kind of sexual love is holy and pure and that God Himself is the author of this love.

2

Human Sexual Anatomy

Ṣadé was a good Christian girl from a deeply conservative background. She had come to associate sex with sin as a consequence of the teaching she had grown up listening to in her parents' church. She told us how this outlook was concerning her more and more with every day that her wedding drew closer. She had never felt comfortable looking at her own naked body, so how was she expected to be comfortable being naked in front of someone else? She had never looked at her own vulva, and now she was expected to let someone else look at it and touch it too?

By the time she reached out to us, she was three months to her wedding. She knew her husband would want to have sex right away—after all, they had both waited so long for this—but she knew that even the thought of him touching her would make her feel dirty, like she had disappointed God and her mother too.

Ṣadé told us about her elder sister's testimony night—the church's equivalent of the hen night or bachelorette party— and how a designated 'auntie' made a big show of admonishing Debìsí, the bride, to be a good wife, to please her husband in every way, and have sex with him anytime he asked for it.

'How is Dẹ́bísí expected to do this when you and Mama and all our other aunties drummed it into our ears that sex was bad?' Ṣadé exclaimed. 'No, Dẹ́bísí and her husband are not going to have sex,' she retorted sarcastically, 'they are going to pray and fast. No grandchildren for you, since you all didn't teach us anything about sex!'

'Mtcheeeew!' she kissed her teeth forcefully, the way only a true Nigerian could.

You see, Ṣadé, and many young Christian women like her are products of their churches' one-sided teaching on sex. They grow up hearing over and over again that sex is bad, and that all sexual desire is of the devil. Virginity is almost elevated to the same position as salvation, and young women go on to believe that their marriages will automatically be successful, so long as they delay sex until they say their wedding vows. Then when they eventually get married, they are somehow expected to miraculously become sexual experts at pleasing their husbands.

The expectation of those who push this teaching is that young women will arrive at the altar, dressed in virginal white and innocent of sin, but the statistical fact is that a worryingly large number do not. The few who toe the line, however, can end up broken sexually and are usually completely ignorant of even the most basic information about sex and sexuality.

Thank God Ṣadé opened up to us! We prayerfully created a treatment plan to help her connect with her sexuality in a way that she was comfortable with, and in a way that helped her honour God and her husband-to-be. As she completed the plan, she was able to rethink sex from a biblical point of view, so that by the time she was walking down the aisle, Ṣadé could now see sex as God's gift to her, something to enjoy rather than fear, and something that gives glory to God.

As we mentioned, part of Ṣadé's initial problem was unfamiliarity with her sexual anatomy because she was never taught about it from a godly perspective. In this chapter, we want to take you to the next step in your journey of discovering wholesome and balanced sexuality by exploring the female and male reproductive systems. Our goal is to fill in the empty spaces left by several decades of silence in the church, and to correct any misinformation you may have learned from secular sources.

When speaking about the topic of sex education on the *Olorì Coitus* podcast, our host, Yésìdé, asked us a very important question: 'Is it really the church's responsibility to teach sex education to the extent that you are advocating? Is this not the role of parents and perhaps the schools?'

Our response was simple. It takes a village to raise a child, and for us as believers, a large part of that community is our brothers and sisters in Christ. Leaving sex education to mainstream schools means we miss out on a key opportunity to reinforce God's word about abstinence, and that we open up our children to the liberal worldview that simply hands kids condoms and tells them to get on with it.

The church has a school too. It's called Sunday school. While we do not necessarily need to teach sex education and human sexual anatomy from the pulpit, it definitely needs to be taught in our youth groups, teenage camps and children's educational classes.

So, if you weren't taught adequate sex education from a healthy perspective or are mostly ignorant of basic sexual anatomy, let's reacquaint you with the different parts of the human external sexual reproductive systems, starting with your own.

Female Sexual Anatomy

Find a quiet, comfortable and well-lit place where you will not be disturbed. Sit with your legs spread, your back supported and your knees open. Use a large mirror with a handle and identify each part as we go along.

Vulva

Everything that is typically considered a part of your external genitalia is the vulva. (Please note that the vagina is mostly internal and cannot be seen without special medical equipment; we'll discuss it in a few pages.)

Mons Pubis

This soft pad of fatty tissue sits just on top of your vulva below the belly button.

There is no direct equivalent of this in males.

Labia Majora and Minora

The labia are the lips of the vulva. They are gatekeepers to the entrance of your vagina.

The first, larger pair of lips are the soft and hair-bearing labia majora. They can be the same shade as the rest of your skin or considerably darker. Both variations are normal. The second, smaller pair of lips are your labia minora. They are usually thinner, pinker and more sensitive and can get larger or smaller when aroused (more on this later).

The labia majora is equivalent to the scrotum in males.

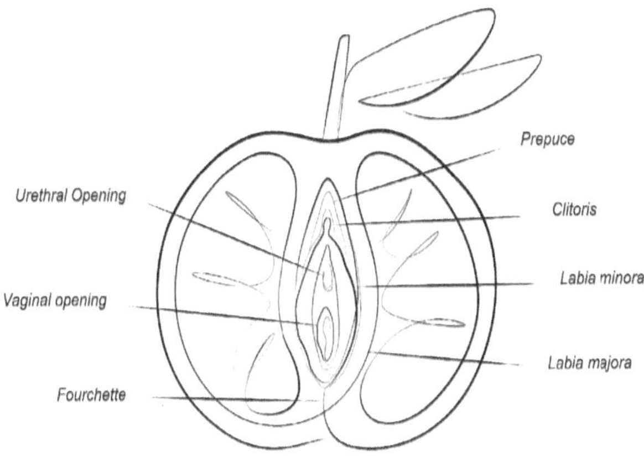

Clitoral Hood (Prepuce)

Your clitoral hood, or prepuce, is the upper junction where labia minora's lips meet. It protects the delicate clitoris, which it envelops almost completely when you are not aroused. During arousal, it retracts gently to unveil the tip of the clitoris.

The clitoral hood is equivalent to the foreskin in males.

Fourchette

Your fourchette is the lower junction where the left and right lips of the labia minora meet—the upper junction being the prepuce. This area can contain several pleasure points, but not everyone finds it pleasurable.

The fourchette is equivalent to the frenulum in males.

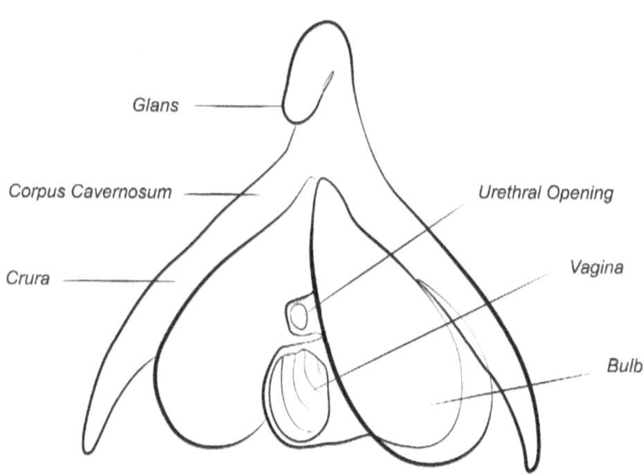

Clitoris

The only part of your clitoris that is visible externally is the clitoral tip, or glans clitoris, which lies just above the top junction of your labia minora, above the opening of the urethra.

The glans clitoris is roughly the size of a pea and is thought to have about 8,000 pleasure-producing nerves. This is about the same number of nerves as there are in the penis but more than three times the concentration per square inch. That's a lot of pleasure!

The rest of your clitoris is hidden beneath the surface. It looks like a wishbone and is a large sensory tissue made up of two identical arms and two bulbs measuring about 8 inches long from tip to tip. Essentially, the glans is just the tip of a much, much larger sexual iceberg.

The clitoris is equivalent to the penis in males.

Hymen

The hymen is a thin piece of stretchy tissue that completely or partially covers the opening (introitus) of your vagina. The hymen is different for every woman. Most hymens will have some form of perforations, ranging from several small holes to one or two larger slits, to allow menstrual blood to pass through.

Some women have no perforations, so their vagina is completely sealed. This is called an imperforate hymen. A closed vagina can't menstruate, so when a girl with this problem reaches puberty, a doctor must perform minor surgery to open the hymen so she can menstruate.

Some women are born without a hymen altogether, and this too is completely normal.

The hymen can break or rupture for many nonsexual reasons like stretching, gymnastics, exercise and horse riding. Because of this, and because not all females are born with a hymen, doctors now agree that the presence or absence of a hymen is *not* a reliable way to determine whether a woman has had penetrative sex or not. Neither is bleeding or the absence of bleeding.

There is no direct equivalent of the hymen in males.

Vagina

Another name for your vagina is the birth canal. This elastic muscular tube serves three purposes: to allow menstrual blood flow, to allow your husband's penis to penetrate during sex and to allow for the birth of your children. The vagina is an internal organ. The part that you can see on the outside is only the entrance, or the introitus.

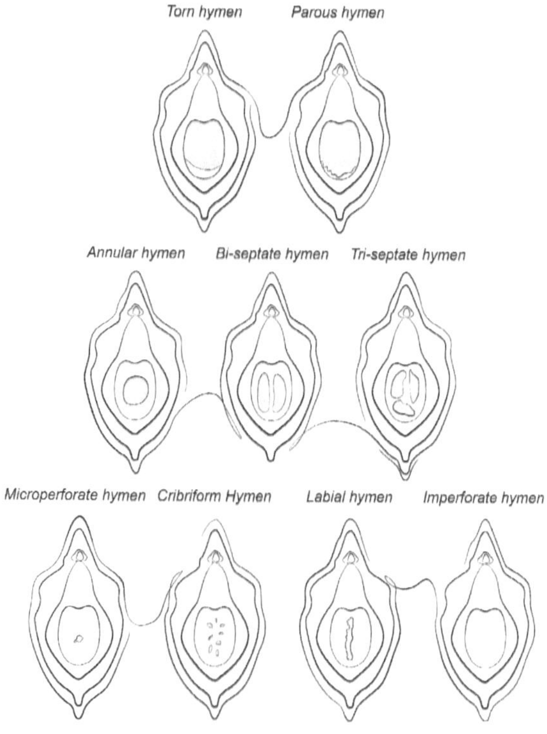

The vagina is about 3 to 4 inches (7.5 to 10 centimeters) long, the size of a credit card. The top and bottom walls are sandwiched together in an *H* shape which keeps the birth canal shut, so that at any given time, your vagina is mostly closed. When your vagina is closed and you are not aroused, its walls are rough and bumpy (like a scrunchie). When you are aroused, your vagina opens up and can stretch out to more than twice its length, becoming smoother inside.

Several glands produce a fluid that lubricates the vagina and keeps it moist and healthy. Lubrication is also necessary for comfortable, pleasurable sex. You should know that most of the pleasure nerves in the vagina are located only in the first third of the canal. We will discuss why this is important in Chapter 9.

G-Spot

The famous G-spot (short for Gräfenberg spot) is not really a spot. It's more so a spongy area just inside the upper wall of the vagina, about 1 to 2 inches (2.5 to 5 centimeters) from the vaginal opening. If stimulated correctly, it can produce an intensely pleasurable sensation. This area is so close to the clitoris that some researchers now think the pleasure sensations derived from stimulating the G-spot actually come from indirect clitoral stimulation.

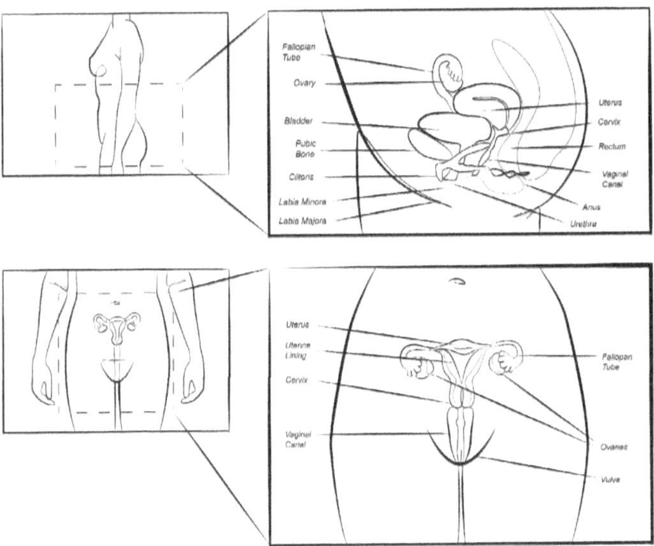

Cervix

The vagina, or birth canal, leads to the womb (uterus). The cervix is the 'neck of the womb' and acts as a gateway to the uterus. The cervix protrudes into the vagina and can be felt as a small nub at the end of the canal. It is always closed, and part of its role is to keep bacteria out of the womb. It opens for only three reasons: to let menstrual blood out of the uterus, to allow sperm to pass from the vagina into the uterus, and to allow a baby to pass into the world from the womb. During sexual intercourse, the cervix can sometimes be stimulated by the tip of the penis, which can be uncomfortable for some women.

Anterior, Lateral and Posterior Fornices

Because the cervix protrudes into the vagina, it creates four 'shoulders' in the corners of the vagina called fornices (*fornix* is singular).

The largest of these is at the back and is called the posterior fornix. During arousal, the muscles of the vagina change shape in a process called tenting, which causes the posterior fornix to lengthen so that deep penetration is more comfortable.

The left and right lateral fornices at the side are shallow and, along with the posterior fornix, serve as reservoirs for sperm, which can survive there for up to five days after sexual intercourse.

The anterior fornix is a small lip at the front of the cervix. It contains an area that is thought to be connected to the clitoris (yes, the clitoris possibly extends that far), and stimulating this 'anterior fornix erogenous zone' can produce intense sexual pleasure and orgasm.

Male Sexual Anatomy

If you have never had sex before, or if you have practiced abstinence, you may not have seen a penis for a long time, perhaps as far back as your childhood, when younger children were innocent enough to play naked together. Well, a lot has changed since then! Let's refamiliarise you—or familiarise you—with the external male sexual anatomy.

Penis

The primary male sexual organ is the penis. Just like vulvas and vaginas, they come in different shapes and sizes, all of which are normal. The penis is infinitely less complicated than a vulva or vagina, but it's an impressive organ nonetheless. It has two states: flaccid (limp) and erect (firm).

Erection is the process in which a limp penis stiffens and becomes hard. Erections happen mostly in response to sexual arousal but can sometimes occur spontaneously without sexual stimulation, especially in the early morning. The penis has two spongy compartments on each side called the cavernosa, which fill with blood when the penis is erect. It's this filling up with blood, much like a balloon filling up with air, that enlarges the penis and makes it hard and stiff.

A penis's size when it is flaccid is not a reliable predictor of its size when erect. This is because penises can be either showers or growers. Showers *show* and growers *grow*

Showers are penises that show or display most of their final erect size even when they're flaccid. Showers get erect by hardening and stiffening but only get slightly bigger.

Growers are penises that display only a fraction of their erect size when they're flaccid. Growers get erect by growing in size as well as hardening. Some growers can quadruple their flaccid size when fully erect.

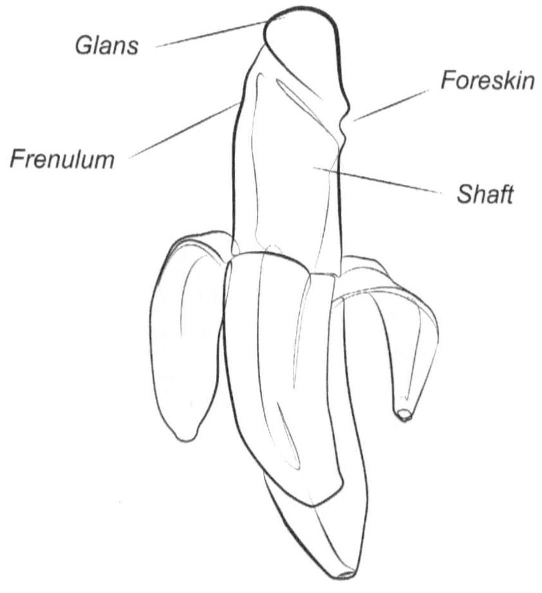

Glans

The bulbous head of the penis is known as the glans penis, or simply glans. It is very sensitive and, like the clitoris, has over 8,000 nerve endings. The nerves in the glans, however, are spread out over a much larger area.

Frenulum

The most sensitive part of the glans is the frenulum.[1] The frenulum is a highly erogenous elastic band of tissue under the glans penis that connects the foreskin to the underside of the penis, and helps the foreskin cover the tip of the penis.

Shaft

The shaft of the penis extends from under the glans to the scrotum. It consists of the insertable length of the male sex organ. There are several variations of penis size and structure, most of which are absolutely normal.

Some penises are straight along the entire length of the shaft (the body of the penis, or the main part). These look mostly symmetrical from both sides. Others curve to the left, right, up or down, which is normal too. It only means that one of the cavernosa is slightly longer than the other, causing the penis to curve in the direction of the shorter cavernosum.

Some penises are larger, and some are smaller. The average penis is about 5 to 6 inches (about 12.5 to 15 centimeters) long and about 4 to 5 inches (10 to 12.5 centimeters) in diameter. The thickness will vary from tip to shaft. Some penises are smooth, and others are bumpier from prominent veins. Both are normal.

Some men have a larger-than-average penis in terms of thickness, length or both. This too is normal. First-time sex with a larger-than-average penis can be a little more daunting, but with adequate preparation and technique, it can be just as fulfilling.

On the other hand, some men have a smaller-than-average penis—also normal. With proper technique and skill, a small penis can be just as effective as an average-sized one.

Foreskin

The foreskin is a flap of tissue that covers the sensitive head (tip) of the penis. If you recall, it's equivalent to the clitoral hood in the female. There are two variations: the circumcised penis—one with no foreskin—and the uncircumcised penis—one with foreskin. Male circumcision is a procedure where the foreskin is removed for religious, cultural or medical reasons. The presence or absence of the foreskin is not thought to negatively affect sexual pleasure or performance.

Scrotum and Testicles

The testicles are walnut-sized organs that hang outside the body between the legs in a skin-enveloped bag called the scrotum. Remember, the scrotum is equivalent to the labia majora in women.

Like labia majora, the shape and size of scrotums and the testicles they hold are very different too. Some are tight and hang close to the body, while some are loose and hang further down between the legs. Some testicles are large, and some are small. The testicles produce sperm and the main male sexual hormone, testosterone.

And there you have it. All of the female and male sexual anatomy in their glorious detail. We feel this part of the journey to fulfilled married sex is very important because the Bible teaches us that when we get married, our bodies are no longer ours alone but are now our spouse's too. Now you know what you have and what you are getting. Wink!

Prayer

Dear Lord, thank You for the wonder of the human body, how You created it with precision and purpose. May my body bring You glory in Jesus's name, amen!

Notes

1. Sorrells ML, Snyder JL, Reiss MD, Eden C, Milos MF, Wilcox N, Van Howe RS, 'Fine-Touch Pressure Thresholds in the Adult Penis', *BJU International*, 99/4 (2007), 864–69, doi:10.1111/j.1464-410X.2006.06685.x

3
Naked and Unashamed

The human body is beautiful, fearfully and wonderfully made (Psalm 139:14, KJV). God created us as a reflection of His glory, in His image and in His likeness (Genesis 1:27).

In Genesis 2:25, the Bible says the man and his wife walked around the garden and were naked and not ashamed. More than just being unclothed, there was an unparalleled intimacy and openness in Eden between Adam and his wife, Eve. They were in harmony with themselves and with God—a harmony that permeated the entire space but was lost after they ate from the tree that God asked them not to. We believe that this level of intimacy and harmony is only attainable when a man and his wife unite in lovemaking, and are once again naked together and unashamed.

After the fall, when innocence was lost, mankind became aware of their nakedness and covered themselves with leaves as they hid from God and from each other. Sin broke the innocence of nakedness and destroyed the intimacy that was once found in it.

Unfortunately, there are countless stories that portray Eve as a temptress who seduced her husband by offering him a bite of the forbidden fruit, leading him away from God's will. In these stories Eve is painted in the same light as Delilah, Jezebel and the foreign wives of Solomon. This portrayal of Eve's supposed seduction, the erroneous belief that sex was the forbidden fruit, and the resulting realisation of human nakedness that followed after they ate the fruit, has pushed the false narrative that the female anatomy is inherently evil and shameful, something to be hidden away at all costs.

But all you need is just a little bit of study to see that it was Adam, not Eve, whom God held responsible for the fall. Read the Genesis story with fresh eyes, and you will see that Adam was standing right there with Eve when she took the fruit, bit into it and ate it. He did not say a word. Then the Bible says she offered it to him and he ate it too. Who is to say that he hadn't wanted it just as much as she did? He didn't resist, he was a wilful participant in the eating, and when the time came to face the Lord, he was quick to throw her under the bus. We can even go as far as to suggest that Adam probably used Eve as a scapegoat,[1] to take the fall for a sin he would have committed were the tables turned.

'It's not my fault. I did nothing wrong. It's Eve's fault and Yours too. You gave her to me, didn't You?'

See, not only did Adam present himself as the righteous victim, but he tried to absolve himself of any responsibility, and even blamed God for *His* failure to defend the paradise he was given to protect.

Nakedness became associated with shame only when innocence was lost. Innocence was lost when sin entered the world. The Bible says in Romans 5:12–21 that sin came into the world through Adam, not Eve.

This is why Jesus came as the last Adam, to undo the damage of sin (1 Corinthians 15:45–48).

Adam denied the blame. Jesus took it.

Adam pointed fingers at everyone but himself. Jesus took the sin of everyone, even though He Himself had no sin.

Adam stood smug and self-righteous.
Jesus bowed humbly and died to give us His righteousness!
Hallelujah!

Now, even though modesty is a biblical requirement for both men and women, it is young girls and women who overwhelmingly find themselves shamed by church culture and Christian society into believing that their bodies are somehow inherently seductive or sinful. We should be teaching our young men self-control; instead, some sections of Christian society demand, enforce even, the total and complete obscuration of the female body, under the guise that even a glimpse of an ankle is seductive and that the girl who bares it is a seductress. Young girls are made to feel that by merely existing, their bodies are seductive magnets for sin and lust. Maybe you heard someone say something like this to you when you were an adolescent:

> *'Your breasts are getting bigger. You must cover up so you don't make that man sin.'*

We believe in true biblical modesty as modelled in 1 Peter 3:1–4, but we reject the doctrine that teaches a special brand of Christian shame that is forced on girls throughout adolescence and into adulthood. When they become mothers, they then pass that shame on to their daughters and their daughters after them. Little girls are erroneously made to believe that they, like Eve, are temptresses and seductresses, who must be curtailed and subdued.

This warped view of modesty has no basis in scripture. Yes, it is true that the unregenerated heart of mankind is wicked and sinful beyond measure (Jeremiah 7:9), and we all, male and female, are capable of immense wrongdoing. It is also vitally important that Christian women do not adorn themselves in a way that attracts lustful attention. But one thing is certain: the nakedness of Adam and Eve (and the female anatomy in particular) was not the cause of the fall. In fact, it was the fall that damaged the purity and innocence of their nakedness, much like it did everything else.

Christian women (and men) are called to be modest in their dressing and presentation, but this is to bring glory to God and to honour the Holy Spirit, whose temple our bodies are (1 Corinthians 6:19). **We do not cover up because our bodies are *sinful*; we cover up because our bodies are *holy*!** Knowing that you carry God inside you is both a great responsibility and an immense honour.

So you see then that in the absence of sin, when sex is done God's way, innocence is preserved and nakedness has no shame. This is only possible in marriage. The ability to be truly naked in a marriage, both physically and emotionally, is paramount for the success of that marriage. Sadly, so many have come to associate their nakedness with sinfulness, and they never experience the fullness of what a truly unashamed marriage could be.

The female body is not sinful. If it was, God would not have chosen Mary as the conduit for Jesus to come into the world. God made the woman specially, crafted her not from dust like He did man, but from flesh and bone. He designed you like a master craftsman makes a royal crown, and when He was done, He looked at His work and said it was very good.

We do not cover
up because our bodies
are sinful; we cover
up because our bodies
are *Holy!*

Your body is a masterpiece, and your sexual anatomy is a sacred part of your body. It is not a taboo. It was created by God to be a vehicle for procreation, a channel for intimacy and an instrument of your pleasure.

Embrace the beauty of how God created you and the precision with which He moulded every curve and marked out every line. Your body is the temple of the Holy Spirit, and He dwells in you!

Prayer

Dear Lord, thank You for making me the way You did, for designing me with expert precision in Your image and in Your likeness. Help me to remember that You created my anatomy and my sexuality, and teach me to know that they too can bring You glory. In Jesus's name, amen!

Notes

1. *Scapegoat*: We opine that Adam probably could have done the same as Eve were the tables turned because in the Biblical narrative, we see him as a silent accomplice, not an unwilling participant.

The concept of the scapegoat is an interesting parallel here. The Jewish ritual is detailed in Leviticus 16:21–22, where we see how the priest would pronounce the sins of Israel onto the scapegoat, and it would take the sins of the people outside the city. Guilt traded for innocence. This was a shadow of Christ, who was taken outside the city to be crucified, and how He took our guilt and exchanged this for His righteousness. God's justice against sin was satisfied by the death of the sinless Son, and we received life and righteousness. Jesus's atonement for our sins was foreshadowed by the laws set out in the old covenant.

4

How You Get Turned On: Buttons, Switches and Levers

Have you ever heard arousal described as being *turned on*? It's an interesting phrase because it brings to mind a light bulb. The light bulb possesses the infinite capacity to radiate heat and light, but its power and brightness remain unknowable until the switch is thrown.

God created your body with an infinite capacity to experience pleasure, and the potential for this pleasure is like the potential of a light bulb. When the switch is thrown, you and the light bulb can experience the true power of what you were created to accomplish.

However, unlike the simple light switch that turns on a bulb, your body is much more complex. It has several buttons, switches and levers, all of which work together to create the physiological sensation of sexual arousal. In the next chapter we will explore why the phrase 'turned on' may be inaccurate, but for now, let's discover where all these sexual buttons are for you. To do this, we will consider the six senses and explore how each of them contributes to arousal. Then we will learn about the different types of touch receptors and erogenous zones.

Six Senses

You have five primary senses: sight, hearing, smell, touch and taste. All of these can turn you on, but the first four are more likely to do so. There's also another sense, a sixth sense, that can create arousal: imagination or fantasy.

Let's try a thought experiment. Think about your husband-to-be. (If you just smiled, then you are doing something right!) Imagine you have been married for a few years, and that you are picking him up from the airport after a long time away abroad. Imagine he is walking towards you from the airport gate a few hundred feet away. In what order do you think your senses would detect his presence?

For most people, it could look something like this:

You already know when his flight lands, and as each second passes, you anticipate him more and more. You get a sense that he is near, and you notice that your **imagination** *is filled with thoughts of him. You crane your neck and stand on tiptoes to peer over the shoulders of the sea of people at the arrivals terminal.*

Immigration cleared, bags finally collected, he makes it through the gate, and then you **see** *him from afar. You notice how he looks, what he is wearing, how he walks. As he gets closer, you see his eyes, his hair, his teeth, his smile, and the masculine curves of his body.*

Soon he is close enough for you to **hear** *his voice. He is calling your name, and it is the most beautiful sound you have ever heard. The tone and timbre of his voice make you weak in the knees; you can't wait for him to come closer.*

*You catch a whiff of him as he gets even nearer; you **smell** his signature perfume mixed with his familiar masculine musk. He opens his arms as you run towards him and fly into his warm embrace.*

*You feel his **touch** as he catches you midair, holds you tight and moves a strand of hair from your face. Wrapped in his tight embrace, you can feel his heart beating, and as he pulls you in tighter, you melt into his arms, feeling safe and sound.*

*Finally, his lips **touch** yours and you **taste** him as he kisses you deeply. When he gives you a gentle peck on your forehead, you smile and relax into his embrace. This is where you know you belong. This is home.*

Which of the six senses felt more real for you? Which gave you the most intense reaction? Rank them in order of importance to you, from 1 star (least important) to 5 stars (most important).

Imagination
Sight
Hearing
Smell
Touch
Taste

When we put this to our focus group, **touch** consistently came up with the most votes, closely followed by **imagination**. This is not surprising because touch and fantasy are the easiest ways to turn most people on. Even so, not all touch is created equal, and not all parts of the body respond the same way to being touched.

Don't worry if touch or imagination did not score the highest marks for you. Sight, sound and smell also play a vital role in sexual arousal. What is important is to know what works for you and to use it to your advantage.

Touch Receptors

There are four main types of touch receptors in your skin. Each respond to different types of stimulation, including sexual stimulation. Some are slow adapting, meaning they keep responding to a stimulus until it's removed, and some are rapidly adapting, meaning they respond quickly to a stimulus when it starts and sometimes when it ends.

Merkel's disks are *slow-adapting* nerve endings that respond to *light touch* and *sustained pressure*. They are found in the upper layers of skin in areas like your lips, fingers and genitals.

Meissner's corpuscles are *rapidly adapting* neurons that respond to *low-frequency vibrations, fine touch* and *changes in texture*. They are located in the skin on your fingertips, the palms of your hands, the soles of your feet, your toes and your eyelids.

Ruffini endings are *slow-adapting* receptors that respond to *skin stretch*. They're found in both hairless and hairy skin across your entire body.

Pacinian corpuscles are *rapidly adapting* receptors located deep in your skin. They respond to *deep pressure* and *high-frequency vibration*. These receptors are located in your hands, feet and breasts. They are also found in blood vessels and joints.

All four of these receptors are low threshold, which means that they don't need a lot of stimulation to respond.

There are several ways to get a response from a touch receptor:

Very light touch
Light touch
Firm pressure
Deep pressure
Vibration
Heat
Cold
Stretch

Let's try another experiment, shall we?

Place your left arm on a flat surface, palm side up. Then hold your right index finger above the surface of your forearm, between your elbow and your wrist. Move it as close as you can to the skin until it almost touches it and hold your index finger in the air as still as you can. (Switch this around if you are left-handed.) Now, very slowly, move your finger even closer, as close as you can, so that you just about feel the sensation of touch. Now stop. Run your finger across your arm a few inches, as lightly as you can without putting any pressure on it.

How close can you place your finger to your arm before you start to feel a sensation in your arm?

Next, from the same starting position, holding your index finger above your forearm, push it deep into your arm, all the way until you can't go any deeper.

How does this feel? Did you notice the point where pressure becomes pain?

Let's try the same experiment again, this time using the palm of your hand instead of your forearm.

Place your arm on a flat surface, palm side up, then hold your right index finger above the surface of your palm. Move it as close as you can to the skin until it almost touches it, and hold your finger in the air as still as you can. Now, very slowly, move your finger even closer, as close as you can, so that you just about feel the sensation of touch. Now stop. Run your finger across your palm to the tip of your middle finger, then to the base of your wrist, as lightly as you can without putting any pressure on it.

How close to your palm can you place your index finger before you start to feel a sensation in your skin?

Now for deep pressure. Hold one thumb above the meaty part of your other palm, just near your wrist, but this time push it as deep as you can, until you can't go any deeper.

How does this feel?

Did the sensation of deep and light touch in your arm and your palm feel different or similar?

Results may vary from person to person, but in general, the participants of our focus group found that applying deep pressure caused mild pain in the arm but not so much in the palm. They also found that light touch was more sensitive in the palm than it was on the arm. Were your results the same or different?

So why does the same level of touch stimulation or intensity of pressure feel different when applied to different parts of your body? It's because the touch receptors are distributed differently across the body, and some areas have more receptors that respond to pain or pleasure than other areas. For example, placing an ice block on your back will create a different response than when it's placed on your lips or your earlobes.

Now you know that your body has a variety of different touch receptors, each responding to varying intensities of stimulation. To fully maximise the potential of each touch receptor, it is essential to experiment with all eight types of stimulation (very light touch, light touch, firm pressure, deep pressure, vibration, heat, cold and stretch). We explore this further in Chapter 9 when we talk about exploratory sex. You now also know that these touch receptors are distributed widely across different parts of your skin, making some areas more responsive to sexual stimulation than others.

You probably already know that a gentle brush against your nipple will create a vastly different response than the same action would on your knee or nose. The nipple is an example of an *erogenous tissue*. There are twenty special areas of your body that respond specifically to sexual touch, and these are called *erogenous zones*. These specialised areas of skin and mucosa (protective inner linings of organs and other body parts) create a complex web of nerves and touch receptors that produce your perception of sexual pleasure, and we discuss these in detail next.

Erogenous Zones

An erogenous zone is an area of the human body that has heightened sensitivity and, when stimulated, creates a sexual response, such as relaxation, sexual fantasies, sexual arousal or orgasms.[1]

Theoretically, any stimulation of an erogenous zone can produce some degree of pleasure in a person who is sensitive to pleasure in that zone *and* who is a willing participant of the stimulation, (except in cases of arousal non-concordance).[2] However, to be able to achieve the most pleasurable response, the receptors in each zone need to be stimulated with the right intensity and using the right type of stimulation.

So it's not just enough for your husband to *touch and kiss and caress* you. He will need to know where and how to touch and kiss and caress you. And how will he know this? That's right! You will need to teach him.

Let's try another experiment. For each of the following erogenous zones, use very light touch, light touch, firm pressure and deep pressure to see if you can identify which of your own zones respond better to a particular type of touch. Write these down in a notebook.

Non-sexual Erogenous Zones

1. Hair and scalp
2. Lips
3. Ears
4. Nape of neck
5. Armpit
6. Inner arm and wrist
7. Palms of hands/fingertips
8. Lower back
9. Belly button
10. Inner thighs
11. Back of knees
12. Soles of feet

After you are done, you should be able to see at a glance what your top erogenous zones are, and what kind of stimulation best works for you.

The other eight erogenous zones are part of your sexual organs. You should wait until you are married to explore these areas with your husband. We will detail them as part of exploratory sex techniques in Chapter 9.

It can seem daunting at first, the numerous buttons, switches and levers that are responsible for turning you on. But don't worry—not everyone will need to experiment with every single item listed in this chapter, and as you may have already discovered, some of them will likely do very little for you.

What is important is knowing yourself and what works for you.

Prayer

Dear Lord, how excellent are the works of Your hands, how marvellous are Your ways. As I prepare my body, mind and spirit for my wedding day and wedding night, I pray You hold me close and lead me aright. In Jesus's name, amen.

Notes

1. 'Erogenous zone', *Wikipedia* (last modified 8 Jul. 2021), https://en.wikipedia.org/wiki/Erogenous_zone, accessed 11 Aug. 2021.

2. *Arousal non-concordance*: It is sometimes possible for a woman who does not consent to sexual activity to feel aroused during said activity. This is known as arousal non-concordance. It is thought that the physiological response to touch does not always correlate with the social context it occurs within. There are cases of women who were raped or assaulted but who showed external signs of arousal, like nipple erection or vaginal wetness. This does *not* mean that these women were enjoying the experience or waived their right to consent.

5

How Your Body Responds: Foreplay, Arousal and Climax

So here is what we have learnt so far. There are six senses: sight, smell, taste, touch, hearing and imagination, and these work together to create the experience of arousal. Of the six, touch is considered by some to be the most important.

There are broadly four different types of touch receptors: Merkel's discs, Meissner's corpuscles, Ruffini endings and Pacinian corpuscles, and each of these respond to different types of stimulation.

There are four different levels of touch intensity: very light touch, light touch, firm pressure and deep pressure. Along with vibration, heat, cold and stretch, these can provide sexual stimulation when applied to an erogenous zone.

There are several erogenous zones, each with a different combination of touch receptors that respond to varying degrees of touch intensity.

Okay, great. Now we are able to properly discuss how to use all this information to help create the maximum sexual advantage for you and your husband.

Foreplay

Foreplay is traditionally defined as any activity a couple engages in before sexual intercourse. *Loveplay* is an alternative term that is gaining acceptance, and although it has the same meaning, it helps introduce foreplay as a pleasurable activity in its own right that does not have to end in lovemaking.

When done properly, foreplay can build up enough sexual tension to give either partner intense feelings of pleasure, satisfaction and even orgasm. Apart from physical pleasure, however, it can also help build a deep sense of closeness and intimacy. The emotional connection created during foreplay often lasts well beyond the bedroom.

Whichever term you choose, foreplay or loveplay is an essential part of lovemaking. It involves skilfully combining the knowledge of **anatomy, physiology** and **psychology** to produce the maximum sexual response and, by so doing, create the most pleasurable experience for you and your husband.

One benefit of foreplay is that it prepares your body for sex by providing the stimulation your vagina requires to become properly relaxed, open and lubricated, which makes it easier for your husband's penis to penetrate without pain or discomfort.

Foreplay isn't just something your husband does to you. Touching, caressing and kissing your husband's body can also enhance your own arousal. One of our clients told us how seeing her husband derive pleasure from her touch and kisses during foreplay boosted her confidence and helped break down her inhibitions, which further enhanced her own sexual pleasure.

Here's what foreplay could look like in a healthy marriage:

Imagine you and your husband waking up on a Friday morning and preparing to go to work. He connects with you emotionally when he draws you in and kisses you good morning. You pray together to set the tone of the day. You get out of bed in your lacy lingerie, and he spanks you playfully on the bottom as you get ready for your shower. He helps get the kids ready for school and blows you a kiss as he hurries out to work.

Throughout the day he sends you memes at work, and a voice note at lunchtime to check on you. He sends a few naughty texts, describing how much he desires you and wants to be with you. You blush uncontrollably at your desk.

When you both get home, he helps out with dinner, and you take turns with bath time and bedtime for the little ones. Children safely in bed, you both cuddle on the sofa, watching television and talking about your day.

Not long after, you feel a familiar hand as he gently caresses the inside of your arms and then moves to your back, firmly massaging the stress of the day away. After a few minutes, he starts softly nibbling at your ear. He knows your buttons and levers (because you have both been open and communicative, and you have taught him how to please you), and he explores your favourite erogenous zones like a master musician playing his favourite instrument. You respond in return, matching each note he plays with a note of your own. By the time you make it to the bedroom (if you manage it at all), you are bursting with desire, and you both make sweet love into the small hours of the night!

As you can see, foreplay is more than just fondling. It involves meeting spiritual, emotional, psychological and physical needs. Foreplay starts way before the sexual act begins and is essential to mentally and emotionally prepare you for sex.

Please know that your husband is not going to know how to do this automatically, even if he has had previous sexual experience. Every woman is different, and what worked for someone else will most likely not work for you. You will jointly need to discover what works for both of you, and you will need to teach each other how you want to be loved.

With foreplay, there is no one-size-fits-all. Because every woman is different, each will respond to the exact same touch in a totally different way. This is why we are not going to prescribe any specific order or pattern to follow. You and your husband are encouraged to explore what feels good and use feedback to create your own repertoire. Take turns touching different areas, focusing on the erogenous zones, using different types and intensity of touch. If it feels good, keep it. If it doesn't, skip it.

We should point out here that the exact same touch might feel one way now and another way later, and something may not feel good initially, only to feel really great as foreplay progresses and arousal heightens. So feel free to try the same things at different times of play to determine whether something is indeed for you or not. For example, aiming straight for the clitoris before kissing or holding each other can feel intrusive, uncomfortable and sometimes even painful. However, after a few minutes of foreplay, the prepuce retracts and the clitoris becomes erect. At this point, directly or indirectly stimulating the clitoris is more likely to produce a pleasurable response.

If it feels good, keep it.
If it doesn't, skip it.

The Phases of Sexual Excitement

So now that you and your husband are in bed or on the couch (or on the kitchen counter, wink) and foreplay is in full swing, let us explore the physiological changes that happen in your body as you get closer to consummating your love.

Sexologists traditionally divide the sexual experience into four distinct phases after the work of Masters and Johnson in the mid 1960s. They are:

Excitement

The sexual excitement stage is also known as the arousal stage. During this time your body begins to make changes that prepare your vagina for intercourse. One of the most recognisable signs of sexual excitement is moistness or even wetness of the vagina. However, because every woman is different and produces varying amounts of vaginal lubrication, the amount of wetness or moistness produced during excitement does not correlate with how much a woman desires sex.

In addition to lubrication, your nipples may get erect, your pupils dilate, your clitoris and vulva swell and change colour as blood rushes to your sex organs.

Plateau

The plateau stage is also known as the build-up stage. During this stage, sexual tension is built up, and just like pressure is stored in a compressed spring, the sexual tension is stored in the nervous system. Every pleasurable sensation adds to the build-up, and the changes you felt in the excitement phase may intensify. The intensity of orgasm is directly related to the amount of tension that is built up in this stage. Some women may notice a change in their breathing, and some may start to vocalise or moan involuntarily. Your vagina may lengthen considerably at this stage, and it is here that deep penetration is most likely to be successful.

Orgasm

The orgasm stage is also known as the climax or colloquially as *cumming*. Orgasm is a release of the tension that builds up during the plateau stage. As we mentioned, enough tension must build up to cross the minimum threshold required for orgasm. When you climax, you may experience a pleasurable sensation, sometimes described as an electric current flowing down your spine, causing involuntary muscular contractions. Your legs may quiver and your hips may pulsate. Your vagina may throb rhythmically, and like some women do, you may release a clear ejaculate fluid or a rush of a creamy vaginal fluid.

Resolution

After orgasm, your muscles relax and your blood pressure drops. Your clitoris might feel particularly sensitive or even painful to touch. Some women may then enter into a short refractory period where they are unable to climax again for a few minutes. Other women may skip the refractory period entirely, and if stimulation continues immediately after orgasm, they may be able to experience multiple orgasms.

New Research

A new theory developed by Dr. John Bancroft and Dr. Erick Janssen, called the Dual Control Model of Sexual Response, helps us further understand how men and women go through each of the four stages of sexual excitement.[1] Drs. Bancroft and Janssen suggest that two opposing systems are constantly at work in our subconscious, both of which control our experience of sexual arousal.

The first part of the system is known as the ***Sexual Excitation System (SES)***, and its role is to promote sexual arousal by responding to thoughts and stimuli that we are conditioned to find arousing.

The second is the ***Sexual Inhibitory System (SIS)***, and its role is to stop the process of arousal. This system protects us from being aroused inappropriately, whether this is feeling turned on in public or feeling aroused by something inappropriate. It expresses itself through personal inhibitions, cultural norms, societal expectations and religious beliefs.

As we mentioned in the last chapter, the phrase 'turned on' is not entirely accurate, because sexual arousal goes beyond getting turned on—it also involves actively 'turning off' your inhibitions, which are a large part of the SIS. Arousal is a blend of both processes, and neither is more important than the other—increasing stimulation for the SES is just as vital as quieting the SIS. They both work together in synergy, just the same way you would put your foot on the accelerator and take your foot off the brakes to move your car.

The theory suggests that women may have a more active inhibition system (SIS) and a less sensitive excitation system (SES) than men. Of course there will be exceptions, but if this is true, then we are to assume that women require more disinhibition—or must lose their inhibition more—to get fully aroused compared to men.

Women have historically always had more to lose from unregulated sexual activity than men (pregnancy, disease, loss of social status), and so it is not unreasonable to see why this might be true. If this is the case, then it may mean that women have a lot more obstacles to overcome from within their own minds to be able to fully experience full arousal and the complete sexual experience.

In our focus group survey, the most commonly reported factors that can completely relax inhibitions were trust and security. How apt! We have preached for years that the best relationship for building trust and security is a long-term, committed marriage.

We recently counselled a newly married lady who was struggling with being intimate with her husband. Fatima explained how sex was becoming a chore for her, because despite almost twenty minutes of foreplay, she was not getting sufficiently aroused or turned on. This meant that her vagina was not wet enough before penetration so every thrust was uncomfortable and left her sore. Fatima was proud of her Fulani heritage, and because Fulani women are known for a high pain threshold, she resigned herself to fate and bore the pain. By the time she was three months into her marriage, she found herself making excuses to avoid lovemaking, and by the time we met her and her husband, they had not had sex in over seven months.

There were several reasons behind Fatima's dilemma. She explained that the culture of northern Nigeria where she and her husband hailed from, believed that the amount of vaginal lubrication a woman produced directly correlated with her desirability or sexual prowess. She told us about an ancient Hausa-Fulani practice called *kayanmata*,[2] which involves using traditional herbs to enhance vaginal lubrication, and how most northern Nigerian Christians frown against its use. Perhaps this is because it is commonly sold alongside other charms, amulets and potions. For Fatima, being a Christian meant that any type of lube was lumped into the same category as kayanmata, and she was reluctant to use anything other than what her body naturally produced.

One other crucial issue we discovered during our sessions with this couple was that although there was foreplay, it was not effective. Fatima's husband, Isa, shared that he had had a long-term sexual relationship several years before he became a Christian. In that relationship, he became accustomed to a certain pattern of foreplay that worked well for his ex-girlfriend, Maryam. Because this pattern always worked, it became reinforced into his subconscious and became the default that he resorted to every time he and his wife had sex. As you might have guessed, nothing that worked for Maryam was working for Fatima. They had different erogenous zones that responded to an entirely different type of touch stimulation.

We started our treatment by explaining the science of vaginal lubrication and assured them that the quantity of natural lubrication produced can vary widely in relation to a woman's level of hydration, the time of the month and other details of her medical history. It turned out that Fatima's vaginal dryness was because she had an undiagnosed medical condition called polycystic ovarian syndrome.

Then we created a program that prompted them to explore the twenty different erogenous zones using each type of touch: very light touch, light touch, firm pressure, deep pressure, vibration, heat, cold and stretch.

In addition, we encouraged Fatima and Isa to explore scripture together, specifically looking at the role of natural aphrodisiacs in the Bible,[3] such as the use of mandrake as part of married lovemaking in Genesis 30:14–16 and Song of Songs 7:13.

Armed with a tube of water-based lube, and a renewed understanding of the way Fatima's body responded to stimulation, they were able to identify each other's most sensitive areas and what type of stimulation worked best for them both. Sex was no longer something Fatima endured, and it became a mutually exciting and pleasurable experience that they both looked forward to.

Your body responds to sexual stimulation in several different ways, and the journey from arousal to climax is different for every woman. You will have your own unique pathway with its own signposts, milestones and divergent roads. Exploring and mapping the terrain of your own sexual pathway can be a lifelong task, because we never really stay static throughout our lives, and we may be constantly changing as we enter new phases and experience new things.

Having a loving and dedicated spouse for the long haul is such a blessing, knowing that they will be there with you as you evolve through the seasons and that they are committed to you, no matter what.

Prayer:

Dear Lord, thank You for making my body the way You did, for placing all the different responses hidden away in different nooks and crannies. May Your truth light the path of my discovery. In Jesus's name, amen!

Notes

1. Kinsey Institute, 'Dual Control Model of Sexual Response', *Kinsey Institute*, https://kinseyinstitute.org/research/dual-control-model.php , accessed 10 Jul. 2021.

2. *Kayanmata*: The Hausa-Fulani tribes of sub-Saharan Africa are known for elaborate wedding fêtes lasting entire weekends. The traditional aphrodisiacs known as kayanmata translate roughly as 'bride's luggage', perhaps to say that they are a crucial part of the things the new bride's mother prepares for her to take to her husband's house. In ancient times the bride's luggage may have also included charms, totems, potions and household idols (similar to the teraphim Rachel stole from her father Laban in Genesis 31).

3. *Biblical aphrodisiacs*: The use of herbs and spices to enhance sexual pleasure and performance is likely as old as civilization itself, and the Bible authors are not shy when it comes to describing their use. Modern-day aphrodisiacs and pharmaceuticals may be more potent but retain the same premise.

6

What to Do When Sex Is Painful

In the last chapter, we brought up several reasons for Fatima's lack of sexual desire. If you recall, one was painful sex due to vaginal dryness, which she discovered was caused by a medical issue. Medical and psychological causes are the two most common reasons for painful sex. Vaginal muscles are often the culprit behind both, particularly psychological.

There are two muscle types in and around the vagina. The vagina itself is a hollow tube of **smooth muscle**, and it is surrounded by several branches of **skeletal muscles** that make up the pelvic floor.

The skeletal muscles *around* the vagina are voluntary, so they can be contracted and relaxed at will. This means that they can be trained like any other muscle in your body.

The **skeletal** muscles in your pelvic floor surround your vaginal opening are the gatekeepers of penetration. One type of skeletal muscle, the bulbocavernosus muscle, works like a sphincter (open and close valve) and needs to be relaxed for successful, pain-free sex.

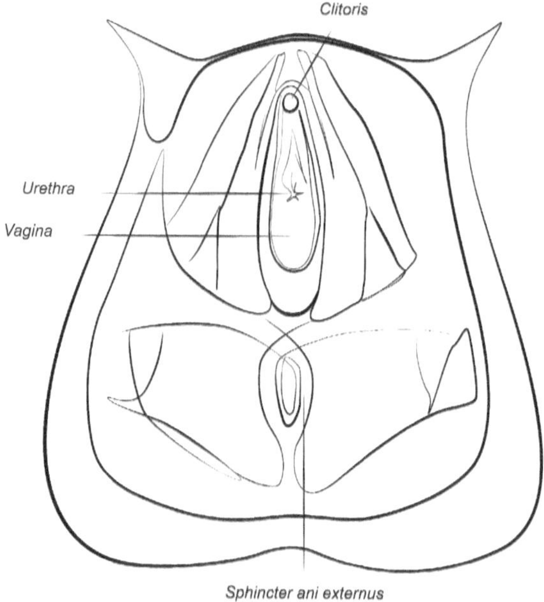

The rhythmic contraction of the other skeletal muscles in the pelvic floor creates pleasure during orgasm. Weak muscles produce a weak orgasm and strong muscles produce stronger orgasms. Since these muscles can be trained, it is possible to strengthen them and by so doing improve the quality and quantity of your orgasms

On the other hand, the **smooth** muscles *in* the vagina are involuntary, so they cannot be controlled at will. These smooth muscles are responsible for changing your vagina's shape during arousal, which allows for deeper penetration and enhances the chances of your husband's sperm fertilising an egg.

Both muscle types play important roles and contribute to normal sexual function, especially when it relates to painful sex. For some women, despite adequate foreplay and relaxation, it can still be very difficult or extremely painful to have sex. The two conditions that account for most cases of painful sex are vaginismus and dyspareunia.

Vaginismus

Vaginismus (vaj-i-NIZ-mus) is a psychological condition that causes the skeletal muscles surrounding the vagina to squeeze shut or spasm involuntarily when vaginal penetration is attempted. This muscle clenching interferes with vaginal intercourse and often results in pain.

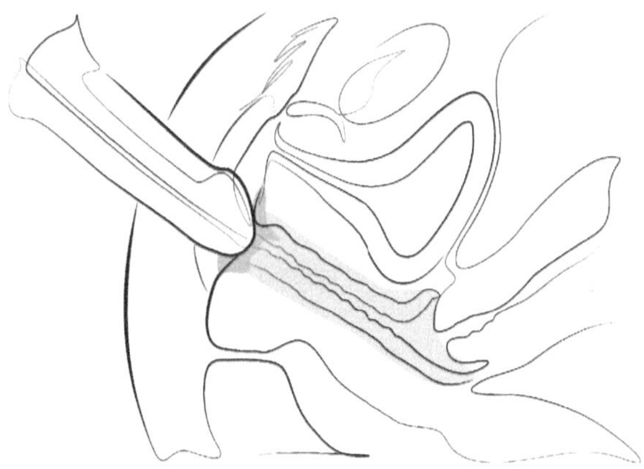

Vaginismus is the external manifestation of an internal fear that penetration will be painful. This fear can be a result of *previous pain* that a woman has **physically** experienced, such as sexual abuse, rape, endometriosis (uterine lining disorder), vaginitis (vaginal inflammation) or episiotomy (childbirth incision), or it could be from an *anticipated pain* due to an **emotionally** or **psychologically** induced phobia. Vaginismus is your body literally putting up a wall of defence to protect you from something that your mind has identified (or misidentified) as a threat. Because of the sensitive nature of this condition, and the fact that many women who have it do not seek medical help, it is very difficult to know how common it is. One study estimates that around 5 to 17 percent of women are affected,[1] but we think the number may be slightly higher due to under-reporting.

Sibongile was a client of ours whom we diagnosed with vaginismus after she was unable to have sex with her husband for over three months after their wedding. She told us how she had been raped by an acquaintance while on a group trip to Cape Town several years before. She did not know her assailant well—he was a friend of a friend—but she knew that she would never forget that night for as long as she lived. It was a trauma she had never spoken of until that afternoon when we sat in a corner of a coffee shop overlooking the docks at Canary Wharf in London.

She had buried the memory deep in the vault of her subconscious, hoping that it would go away, but when her husband tried to make love to her after their wedding, all the memories came flooding back. Muscles she did not even know she had tightened up in defence and shut her husband out to protect her from ever being violated again. The trouble was, this was not an assailant, this was her husband whom she loved. Her conscious mind knew this, but her subconscious mind refused to acknowledge this truth; it believed every man was wicked and brutal, and all it knew was the sharp knife held to her neck and the threats to slit her throat if she made a sound or ever told anyone.

Sibongile is not alone. Several women have experienced some sort of trauma that affects their ability to properly enjoy sex with their husbands. The good news is that there are very effective treatments for vaginismus, and most women can make a full recovery.

For Sibongile, we tackled the fear from its root. We developed a focused Bible study devotional with specific prayer points that targeted her fear **and** combined this with evidence-based, trauma-focused cognitive behavioural therapy, pelvic floor relaxation and gradual vaginal dilation therapy.

The Bible says:

> By his wounds you have been healed.
>
> 1 Peter 2:24, NIV

> I prayed to the LORD, and he answered me. He freed me from all my fears.
>
> Psalm 34:4

If you feel you may have a fear of sexual penetration for whatever reason, please seek medical and psychological advice as soon as possible from a general practitioner, a sex therapist or a psychologist.

Dyspareunia

While vaginismus has psychological causes, *dyspareunia* (dis-pe-ROO-nee-uh) is painful sexual intercourse due to medical causes. In dyspareunia, there may be sufficient vaginal dilation to allow for penetration, but there is pain with each thrust, or sometimes just even the penis being in the vagina can be painful. There are two main types of dyspareunia: shallow (or superficial) and deep.

In shallow dyspareunia, the pain is either on a small portion or all over the surface of the vulva. It may also be felt in the first few inches of the vaginal canal.

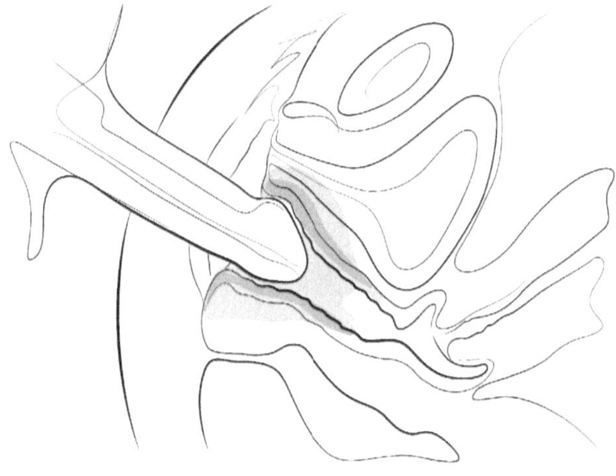

In deep dyspareunia, the pain occurs further inside the vagina, when there is deep pressure against the cervix or when the penis makes contact with any of the fornices (remember from Chapter 3, the shoulders in the corners of the vagina). Some women might also experience deep pelvic pain that extends towards the back and sides.

There are several causes of dyspareunia, ranging from vulvodynia (chronic pain of the vulva) to urinary tract infection, pelvic inflammatory disease, fibroids, ovarian cysts, polycystic ovaries, endometriosis and vaginal dryness, to name a few.

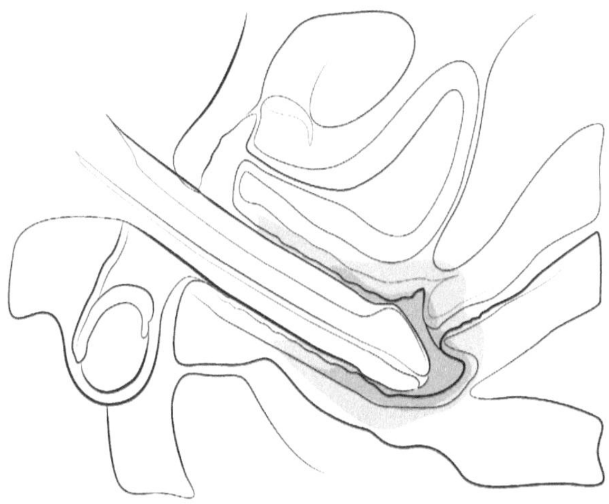

The depth of penetration required to produce pain, the location of the pain and the duration of symptoms all help your clinician determine the diagnosis (along with a thorough medical history, physical examination and relevant investigations).

If you have pain during sex, even if it is your first time, but most especially if the pain develops after months or years of pain-free sex, then we strongly advise that you seek medical advice as soon as possible from a general practitioner, family physician or gynaecologist.

Kegel Exercises

Kegel exercises were developed by Dr. Arnold Henry Kegel and are scientifically proven to strengthen the pelvic floor, heighten sexual pleasure and improve orgasms.

If you have been diagnosed with vaginismus, you should avoid doing kegel exercises as these could worsen your spasms. The treatments for vaginismus include pelvic floor relaxation and vaginal dilation. We discuss vaginal dilation therapy briefly in Chapters 8 and 9.

The first step in doing kegel exercises is to identify your pelvic floor muscles and learn how to isolate them. We all use our pelvic floor muscles daily, but we may not even realise it. Have you ever needed to stop the flow of urine midstream? The muscles you use to do this are the exact muscles you want to train.

Here's how it works: Imagine you have a straw in your vagina and you want to use that straw to suck up some water. The muscles you tighten to complete the sucking motion are your pelvic floor muscles. Try doing three to five contractions—or tightening these muscles three to five times—and hold them for as long as you can, then relax them.

For best results, focus on tightening only your pelvic floor muscles. Don't flex the muscles in your abdomen, thighs or buttocks, and make sure you breathe in and out throughout the exercise; avoid holding your breath.

The *mind-muscle connection* is a term commonly used by weightlifters and bodybuilders to describe the mental connection required to activate a muscle that might be dormant or passive in normal daily activities. Because these muscles aren't typically active, they are not so easy to contract or relax at will.

Building a powerful mind-muscle connection for your pelvic floor will not only improve your sex life tremendously but also help prevent urinary problems that are common in later life as a result of childbearing.

Incorporate kegels into your daily routine, ideally three sets of ten to twenty repetitions every day. The pelvic floor muscles are a vital part of every woman's sexual health, so do yourself a favour by strengthening the muscles that are most intimately tied to your sexuality.

Prayer

Dear Lord, I pray for all women who have experienced trauma or pain that has caused sexual intimacy difficulties with their husbands. Please touch their hearts and heal them, and may they find true and lasting peace. In Jesus's name, amen!

Notes

1. Spector IP, Carey MP, 'Incidence and Prevalence of the Sexual Dysfunctions: A Critical Review of the Empirical Literature', *Archives of Sexual Behaviour*, 19/4 (1990), 389–408, doi: 10.1007/BF01541933. PMID: 2205172

7

Joyful Anticipation vs Lustful Longing

Despite what you may have heard, a good sex life is not a reward for abstinence, the same way a good marriage is not a reward for serving the Lord in your youth. Yes, an abundance of grace smoothes the way and makes things easier when you are led by God's spirit, but it would be unbiblical for us, or anyone, to tell you that all you have to do is fold your arms and pray, and presto! Your sex life is amazing.

It turns out that a good sex life and a good Christian marriage require hard work to build and even more hard work to sustain.

Lauren Meeks was a good Christian girl who was raised in the church. When she was 15 years old, she and a handful of her Sunday School friends made a promise not to have sex until marriage after hearing a talk about abstinence at her church's youth group. Based on the church's unspoken premise, she assumed that remaining chaste would automatically grant her an incredible sex life. Unfortunately, when her wedding night arrived, she realised that the fairy tale she was expecting was anything but, and instead she was faced with some of the 'darkest months of [her] life'!

Lauren shared her story with *Good Housekeeping* magazine in her 2016 article titled 'After Staying a Virgin until Marriage, I Couldn't Have Sex with My Husband'. In it she described how being raised in the church exposed her to an unbalanced teaching about sex and sexuality.

She writes:

> The sexual tension between my fiancé and I certainly didn't make keeping our lips apart or our hands off each other easy. But we had both decided that we wanted to honor each other and honor our God, and so for us the sacrifice was worth it. We were looking forward to sharing that intimacy once we were married. I innocently assumed that all of that work on both our parts to remain chaste would pay off with a hot, passionate sex life after we had finally said 'I do.' I assumed this *because no one had ever told me differently.*[1]

This tension between having desires that were natural and persistent, and being told that those desires were sinful and must be avoided at all costs, created a disconnect in her subconscious which unfortunately led to her developing vaginismus.

Despite several attempts at trying over 'a week of tears and pain and frustration', Lauren and her husband were still unable to consummate their marriage. They had to seek professional help:

> After talking with doctors and therapists, I began to realize that decades of 'saving myself' had subconsciously convinced me that sex was actually bad, something to be avoided and not thought about. And now that it was 'good', my body didn't know what to do.

Lauren was told simply to not have sex instead of being taught why God asked us not to. Neither she nor her husband had had experience with sex, and their sex education at school wasn't adequate. Even though Lauren asked again and again what she should expect on the wedding night, everyone—friends, family and even doctors—told her not to worry and that she would figure it out.

Her church family failed her by its silence. Even though she did exactly as she was told, she ended up hurt and discouraged as a result.

The beautiful part of Lauren's story, however, is that she was able to get help, and despite her ordeal, she did not lose her faith:

> If I had to do it again, I still would have waited. For all of my struggles, I do not regret being raised in a Christian home, and I still have a strong faith. But I would have encouraged—and even demanded—open conversations about the many good aspects of sex and intimacy, rather than being told over and over again to simply avoid it until marriage.

Lauren was hurt by the silence that is prevalent in the church's purity culture because she toed the line. But even those who rebel against the establishment can be directly and indirectly hurt too. Remember the saying about telling someone not to think about elephants? The constant messages to young people to *not* think about sex often means that there is only one thing on their minds. Combine this with the raging hormones of adolescence and the newfound freedom of university, and it is easy to see why the average age of sexual debut in Christian women coincides with starting higher education.

Purity Culture

Because we are silent in the church about sex, there is a huge vacuum of information that needs to be filled.

Unfortunately, the information young people in the church find to fill this gap, and the experiences that come with it, are often steeped in misinformation, gleaned from questionable sources and shrouded in shame and taboo.

The evidence shows that the church's preference for 'abstinence only' sexuality education has had the exact opposite effect of what it was intended to create. Those who save themselves for marriage in response to fear rather than as a natural consequence of their relationship with Jesus can very often become scarred by the process. Not only that, but several studies have shown that 'virginity-focused', abstinence-only teaching is overwhelmingly unsuccessful in preventing sex before marriage.[2] Instead, the research shows a comparative number and sometimes an increase in unmarried sexual activity within the church compared to secular society.[3]

Perhaps like many young Christians, you grew up hearing that sex is sinful, and so you have learnt to feel shame when you are aroused. This shame can be internalised over several years, so that when you are finally allowed to have sex, the damage to your sexuality has already been done. This shame plays a huge role in activating the Sexual Inhibitory System (SIS), as we described in Chapter 5, and can make arousal difficult to sustain. By sabotaging your sex drive, it prevents you from enjoying fulfilling sexual intimacy with your husband.

While it is true that not every young person who grows up hearing these teachings will be affected negatively, far too many have been sexually handicapped for the truth to be ignored: virginity-focused, abstinence-only teaching—a pillar of the church's purity culture—has done more damage than good.

So, what should the church do? Should we be like the secular world and discard abstinence as old-fashioned and instead encourage liberality by promoting sex before marriage?

Absolutely not, God forbid!

Not only is saving sex for marriage God's command, but abstinence has been proven to be the only 100 per cent effective way to prevent unwanted pregnancy, sexually transmitted diseases and abortion.[4]

We do not need to throw out the baby with the bathwater. What the church needs to do is replace the incomplete, abstinence-only sex education with a robust and well-rounded biblical sexual education that informs young people while teaching them God's word that admonishes them to save sex for marriage.

By now you may have figured that this is personal. You see, a large part of our early ministry through the Dianoia Foundation, a campus Christian organisation dedicated to teaching abstinence, was all about promoting purity culture. For over a decade (2001-2012), thousands of 'Purity Promise' cards were distributed to dozens of schools across Ibadan, in southwest Nigeria, and we and our team hosted several conferences, seminars and workshops teaching abstinence until marriage. We are grateful for the impact of this ministry and have received several beautiful testimonies from people who were blessed by it. But because we taught only virginity, not biblical sexuality, we might have inadvertently caused those who listened to us to believe that sex is bad.

It was not until late 2015 when we were researching the findings of the US committee on funding for church-based abstinence-only sex education programs that we discovered the unintended consequences of virginity-focused purity teaching.

Today our non-profit, the Craig Christian Center, offers training, therapy and counselling to men and women who have grown up in purity culture, helping them navigate true biblical sexuality the way God intended. We are not alone, though; there are several other organisations headed by pastors and other Christian leaders who also teach biblical sexuality in full, and together we work to educate other pastors on this holistic approach.

So, how does the church hope to bridge this gap? How can we raise a generation of women who have a wholesome relationship with sex but still choose to honour God by saving sex for marriage? The only way is to teach biblical sexuality for what it is, the kind we see in Proverbs and Song of Songs, while at the same time reinforcing the truth of God's word regarding abstinence.

We must resist the temptation to skim the surface by telling teenagers simply not to have sex, because leaving it at that leaves room for all manner of half-truths and misinformation.

Instead:

We must tell them that sex is good, but only when it is done at the right time.

We must encourage them to look forward to a time when they can righteously enjoy sex.

We must teach women to celebrate their bodies instead of seeing them as instruments of seduction or sin.

We must teach our girls that sex is not something to be ashamed of, but something to rejoice in with the husband that God will one day bring them to.

We must remind them that God reserved sex for marriage, not because it is evil and sinful, but because it is good and righteous.

And we must help the faithful differentiate between lust, desire and arousal.

Lust, Desire and Arousal

Lust is a *strong and often overwhelming attraction for something you don't have or is not yours.* Lust can be used to describe a longing for luxury clothes, cars, jewellery or money, but it is more commonly used to describe the intense sexual attraction that occurs between a man and woman who are not married. Sexual lust is a raging fire that burns ferociously and out of control, igniting anything in its path. Almost everyone has experienced lust at one time or another, however briefly, and most can recognise the intense feelings that come with it.

Lust is a sin.

Our position on lust is simple. *Run!*

The Bible says:

> Can a man scoop a flame into his lap and not have his clothes catch on fire?
>
> Proverbs 6:27

> Flee from sexual immorality. Every other sin a person commits is outside the body, but the sexually immoral person sins against his own body.
>
> 1 Corinthians 6:18, ESV

So flee youthful passions and pursue righteousness, faith, love, and peace, along with those who call on the Lord from a pure heart.

> 2 Timothy 2:22, ESV

Desire, on the other hand, is just as strong and passionate as lust, but one big difference is that the object of desire could be someone you are legally and spiritually covenanted to. Desire is what the lovers in the Song of Songs had for each other:

I belong to my beloved, and his desire is for me.

> Song of Songs 7:10, NIV

Desire is holy.

Arousal is the pleasurable physiological reaction that lust or desire can produce in your body, and this reaction can often be heightened by sexual stimulation. In the bible there are several examples of holy arousal and sinful arousal.

My beloved extended his hand through the opening, And my feelings were aroused for him.

> Song of Songs 5:4, NASB

You (Israel) engaged in prostitution with the Egyptians, your sexually aroused neighbors, multiplying your promiscuity and provoking me to anger

> Ezekiel 16:26 NET

Arousal is neutral.

Arousal is not automatically sinful! When holy desire produces arousal, then that arousal can lead to lovemaking between husband and wife, which is holy. On the other hand, when sinful lust produces arousal, that arousal can lead to sinful fornication or adultery.

We are seeing an increase in the number of female clients who have physiologically shut down every feeling of arousal, mistaking their natural bodily responses for sin, so that when the time comes for them to have sex with their husbands, their minds have already associated erect nipples and vaginal wetness with sin. It takes intensive therapy to reconfigure the subconscious mind to accept that arousal is just a normal physiological response that was put in the body by God, who is the author and creator of sex, and who designed it to be enjoyed.

Have you ever wondered why we see in colour, or why food tastes so good? Do you think you would bump into things or be unable to recognise faces if your colour vision were turned off and you could only see in black and white? Or did you ever wonder if the nutrients in your food would be less sustaining and nourishing if food had no taste? Likewise, sex did not have to be pleasurable. You could get pregnant just as easily if all it took was a twenty-second insemination that felt like a sneeze or a dull rubbing against your knee, but God decided to pack over 8,000 pleasure nerves in your clitoris alone!

All these things—colour vision, taste in food and pleasure in sex—are not strictly necessary for the functions they serve, but God in His wisdom created them for our pleasure, just as He created us for His.

> Thou art worthy, O Lord,
> to receive glory and honour and power:
> for thou hast created all things, and for thy pleasure,
> they are and were created.
>
> Revelation 4:11, KJV

Lust is a sin.
Desire is holy.
Arousal is neutral.

Most pastors know the difference between lust and desire. Perhaps they are reluctant to teach it because they fear that their congregations are not mature enough to understand the difference. Perhaps like the early church,[5] they are worried that telling people all their sins were already paid—including sins of lust—would cause them to do whatever they wanted to do, disregarding Paul's admonishment to stop sinning and live new lives in Christ (Romans 6:1–4). So they gloss over it, keeping quiet and perpetuating the culture of silence.

If the church can teach about sexual desire by conveying the proper time to *bud, blossom and bloom*, however, we believe that we will then be able to differentiate healthy biblical sex from unhealthy, lust-driven sex.

Budding, Blossoming and Blooming

As you know, we must be careful not to confuse lust with desire and arousal. Avoiding lust at all costs is scriptural, but shutting down desire and arousal can lead to serious problems in a marriage.

Desire is only holy when it is directed at something that is yours, right? What happens when the object of your desire is not yet yours, but is going to be? The Bible tells us that there is a time to embrace and a time to refrain from embracing (Ecclesiastes 3:5b). In the Song of Songs, the maiden warned the daughters of Jerusalem:

> Promise me, O women of Jerusalem,
> not to awaken love until the time is right.
> Song of Songs 8:4

There is a time and a place to encourage desire. You see, *timing* is key. We could easily read the passage from Song of Songs 8:4 as, 'Promise me, O women of Jerusalem, that when you awaken love, you will only do it when the time is right'. The scripture is clear that desire is holy in marriage between a man and his wife, but the Bible also seems to suggest, at least in the case of the betrothed and her beloved, that even though they were unmarried, they had reached a point where it was *kosher* for them to allow desire to **bud**, then **blossom** and finally **bloom**, in that order. The reference to flowers is intentional because this is the exact imagery used in scripture.

> Come, my love, let us go out to the fields
> and spend the night among the wildflowers.
> Let us get up early and go to the vineyards
> to see if the grapevines have **budded**,
> if the **blossoms** have opened,
> and if the *pomegranates* have **bloomed**.
> There I will give you my love.
>
> Song of Songs 7:11–12 (emphasis ours)

We teach our clients that desire is good, but it is reserved. There is a right time, right person and right place. Ignite desire sooner than is appropriate, and it can engulf and destroy. Set it in motion at the right time, and desire can be a beautiful and cosy fire that gives off warmth and light for a lifetime.

When we were faced with the question about what time frame we would prescribe for a couple to begin to cultivate desire before the wedding day, we were unable to find any consensus from scripture. We knew we could not leave that question unanswered; otherwise, singles or couples who were not yet at the right place in their journey might arouse desire before its time by reading this material.

As we mentioned at the beginning of this book, we have chosen to present this material, and by extension the budding of desire, to women who are at least three months away from their wedding. However, this is not a biblical injunction, it is merely a poetic expression. This is not entirely arbitrary because we chose the blooming interval of pomegranate flowers in honour of the Song of Songs 7:12 passage you just read.[6]

Everyone is different, and each person's needs will vary, so we strongly recommend that every woman who chooses to use this book should do so with guidance and supervision from a trusted mentor or pastor or her premarital class facilitator.

Joyful Anticipation Therapy

Remember our client Ṣadé? The one who threatened her mother and aunties with no grandchildren? You would be pleased to know that her mum is now a grandma to Ṣadé's two lovely boys. She told us she was sure her marriage would have been vastly different had she not completed our joyful anticipation program.

To treat Ṣadé, we combined evidence-based desensitisation therapy with the principle of joyful anticipation from the Song of Songs to create an eight-week program of prayer, music and meditation. This technique helped slowly transition her from feeling shame when she felt aroused (which led to her SIS automatically shutting down desire) to feeling joy and gladness.

The first thing we did was help her differentiate lust (which is sin) from desire (which is holy). We completed a seven-day deep dive into the book of the Song of Songs and dissected the historical perspective of its Jewish authors. Once we were able to establish that the object of Ṣadé's desire and the source of her arousal was her husband-to-be, and that the anticipation she was building was directed towards the righteous union of her spirit, soul and body with the man God had destined for her, we were able to move on to the next phase.

Over the next six weeks, Ṣadé set aside thirty minutes a day for desensitisation therapy. She would start with a Bible study devotional and a series of prayer points that we had recommended. Then she would sit outside or take a walk in her garden while playing a specific piece of instrumental gospel music overlaid with scripture verses from Song of Songs. We encouraged her to think about her husband-to-be during this exercise using these verses from the Song of Songs, to imagine herself as the betrothed and her fiancé as the beloved, and rejoice in the poetry and imagery as she joyfully anticipated the day when she would be able to righteously make love to him. The aim of this exercise was to provoke arousal without shutting down.

One key aspect of this treatment was the music, which we also use for other clients' treatment plans. Associating the music with feelings of relaxation and arousal creates a mental circuit in the subconscious. If a client does the treatment correctly, playing this music on the wedding night helps usher the couple into a relaxed and peaceful place, opening the floodgates of heaven!

By the third week, Ṣadé told us during our debriefing sessions that she was starting to notice a change in her reaction to arousal and that it was no longer as difficult to sustain. She remarked that the music made it easier to relax and the scripture was a constant reminder that her desire for her husband, just like that of the lover and her beloved, was holy and pure.

By the time we reached the end of the sixth week, Ṣadé was as excited as her fiancé to get to their honeymoon suite. Thankfully, just as we had designed it, by this time their wedding was only a few weeks away.

We finished the program with a week of prayer and fasting, taking the time to praise God for His restoration and for the gift of sexual intimacy in marriage.

In our practice, we use joyful anticipation as a part of desensitisation therapy, and have found it immensely beneficial to our clients. For people who suffer from vaginismus or who have difficulty experiencing arousal, it can make getting aroused and relaxed easier on the wedding night. It also makes first-time sex easier by training our clients' emotions to respond joyfully to their spouses rather than fearfully.

Practicing joyful anticipation is not for everyone. Some people don't need to coax their minds or reset faulty thinking, and some people may find it too difficult to resist the urge to experiment sexually before marriage, due to the intense passion that joyful anticipation can create. It is for this reason that we provided support, supervision and counsel for Ṣadé and all our other clients every step of the way.

It is not advisable to embark on this journey unsupervised, so please speak to your pastor or Christian sex therapist before starting this or any form of sexual desensitisation therapy.

Prayer

Dear Lord, as I approach my budding, blooming and blossoming season, help me not to awaken desire until the time is right. In Jesus's name, amen!

Notes

1. Meeks, Lauren, 'After Staying a Virgin Until Marriage, I Couldn't Have Sex with My Husband', *Good Housekeeping*, https://www.goodhousekeeping.com/life/relationships/advice/a37617/i-waited-to-have-sex-until-i-was-married/, accessed 11 Aug. 2021.

2. Brückner H, Bearman P, After the Promise: The STD Consequences of Adolescent Virginity Pledges', *Journal of Adolescent Health*, 36/4 (2005), 271–78, doi: 10.1016/j.jadohealth.2005.01.005. PMID: 15780782

3. Paik A, Sanchagrin KJ, Heimer K, 'Broken Promises: Abstinence Pledging and Sexual and Reproductive Health', *Journal of Marriage and Family*,78/2 (2016 Apr. 1), 546–61, doi: 10.1111/jomf.12279. Epub 2016 Jan 4. PMID: 27019521. PMCID: PMC4806393

4. 'Abstinence as a Birth Control Option', *Birth Control*, https://birthcontrol.com/options/abstinence/, accessed 26 Aug. 2021.

5. *Silence in the church*: The medieval church in Europe faced a similar dilemma regarding grace. At this time, the Bible was only available in Latin, and the vast majority of the faithful were illiterate. Those who could read did not have access to the scriptures because the painstakingly handwritten copies of the Bible were too valuable and very scarce.

Even though scripture affirms that while we were yet sinners, Christ's righteous act of obedience to death on the cross resulted in justification and life for all people (Romans 5:18) and that the righteousness we now lay claim to was not one borne of works, but by faith, the prevailing understanding of the time was that a person's work put them in good standing with God.

It took a schism to bring change, but the Reformers boldly declared that *we are saved by grace alone, by faith alone and in Christ alone* (Ephesians 2:8–9)! We now know that works cannot produce salvation. *We do not do good works so that we can be saved; we are saved, and because of this salvation, we do good works. The acts of our hands are a reflection of the salvation in our hearts.*

6. Thompson Y, Marisa, 'Pruning Pomegranates', *New Mexico State University, College of Agricultural, Consumer, and Environmental Sciences*, https://aces.nmsu.edu/ces/yard/archives/032319.html, accessed 11 Aug. 2021.

8
First-Time
Sex for Virgins

Affiong was a few weeks to her wedding when she reached out to us on Instagram one cold autumn morning in 2016. Her question was the seed for this book, as mentioned in the introduction, and is one we have been asked several times since, by women who have never had sex:

Does it have to be painful? Am I going to bleed?

If you too have never had sex before and your first sexual experience will be with your husband, you may have similar questions, and you may have heard the same stories she heard. Stories about sex being painful, about there being lots of blood and tears and sweat, and about sticky-icky fluids and embarrassing farts that ruin the entire experience forever.

Nothing could be further from the truth. First-time sex can be beautiful and memorable, and it can set the stage for many more years of exciting lovemaking.

Pain

So let's talk about pain. We believe that no woman should have to experience pain during sex.

Painful sex happens for only four reasons:

1. Medical conditions

2. Psychological reasons

3. An impatient and inexperienced lover

4. An unprepared bride

We have already explored a few medical and psychological conditions that make sex painful and how to treat them. If you have not yet read Chapter 6, you should go back and read that now.

We hope your husband-to-be is going to read the next chapter with you, in addition to the companion to this book, which we have written just for men. If he does, then he should be up-to-date on the basic skills required to ensure a relatively pain-free experience.

Assuming the first three have been taken care of, then all that is left is you. What do *you* need to do to prepare for first-time sex, to make sure that it is nothing like the horror show most people fear and more like the blissful experience we know it can be? That's what this chapter is for!

Bleeding

Just as pain is not a given for first-time sex, neither is bleeding. Remember we discussed in Chapter 3 that the hymen can be stretched or torn by nonsexual means, possibly long before you first have penetrative sex. If this is you, then you are un-likely to bleed very much on your wedding night. The same is true even if your hymen is intact.

First-time sex can be beautiful and memorable, and it can set the stage for many more years of exciting lovemaking.

Based on our experience, when a woman has excessive pain and bleeding at her sexual debut in the absence of any medical or psychological issues, it is more likely to be from a vaginal laceration. Vaginal laceration during first-time sex can be due to improper technique, lack of lubrication or a rough and impatient partner.

Not keen on bleeding on the sheets when you first have sex? Get your husband to stretch rather than tear your hymen using the Craig Technique we will discuss shortly. This way you are less likely to bleed heavily or feel excessive pain.

Vaginal Dilator Therapy

Vaginal dilation is a great way to prevent vaginal lacerations. It works by gently stretching the vaginal walls in preparation for penile penetration using medical-grade cylindrical or cone-shaped devices that come in different sizes. By advancing from the smallest size to the larger sizes, you train your vaginal muscles and prevent spasms.

Some other reasons a clinician might advise dilator therapy are vaginismus, dyspareunia, vulvodynia, vestibulitis (painful vaginal inflammation), pelvic pain, pudendal neuralgia (chronic pain from pelvic nerve damage), difficulty having a gynaecology examination, inability to insert tampons and lichen sclerosus (skin condition with white patches near the genitals).

We advise that you only use dilators under medical supervision to prevent perforation injuries. Please speak to your family doctor or sex therapist to schedule a consultation to see if dilator therapy is right for you.

We explore this and in more detail in the HIGMT workbook which is available on our website.

The Craig Technique: Progressive Fatigue for Comfortable First-Time Sex

If your first sexual experience will be on your wedding day (or if you have been abstinent for a long period of time), here are our suggestions on how to go about making love for the first time:

First off, **set the mood**. Remember the song you played during your six weeks of joyful anticipation? Now is the time to play it. Turn up the volume on your smart speaker and fill the room with music. We suggest keeping the lights on for your first time because your husband will need to see where he is going. Soft light is more flattering, so candles or tea lights might come in handy. If you live in a tropical country or are honeymooning in one, please be aware that fans can dry out your vagina during sex, undoing several hours of foreplay. If it is too hot to keep a fan off, try angling it away from your vagina. Some couples tell us that they prayed a brief prayer before they had sex for the first time. We think this is an excellent idea!

Start with foreplay. Lots and lots of it. Use this as an opportunity to introduce your husband to your body. Take him on a journey to meet every curve and crevice and mound. Use different types of touch. Tell him what feels good, tell him what doesn't. Verbal communication ('yes,' 'right there,' 'just like that') works just as well as non-verbal communication (gasping, moaning, gently guiding his hand or lips to the places you want him to linger). What is important is making sure that your message is received clearly. Allow yourself to become fully aroused and fully relaxed, and then reinforce this state of relaxed arousal by exploring your husband's body in return.

When you feel ready, then it's time to **attempt penetration**. You will know you are ready when you feel moistness or wetness build between your legs, when your vagina starts to pulse gently or when your hips start to rock rhythmically. Get your husband to apply some lubricant to your vulva and vagina. For some women, lubricant application can further increase the feeling of arousal. The more lube you use, the better. Water-based lubricants are best for condoms, but if you are not using one (see our notes on contraceptives in the next chapter), then oil-based lubes work just as well.

Now here is the secret to painless penetration. The Craig Technique is based on a principle called progressive muscle fatigue. Most muscles can be actively squeezed or clenched tightly for only a brief period of time, after which they spontaneously relax. Try it! Shut your eyes as tight as you can. How long can you keep them *tightly* closed? Most people can manage a few seconds before their eye muscles spontaneously relax. The goal of the Craig Technique is to help relax your vaginal muscles by timing penetration with the spontaneous relaxation of your pelvic floor muscles after you have fatigued them.

This type of muscle tightening is different from the involuntary spasms that characterise vaginismus, which we covered in Chapter 6. If you think you might have vaginismus, please speak to a sex therapist or your general practitioner. *Do not* attempt this technique as it will not be effective for you and will likely make the condition worse. Patients with vaginismus need pelvic floor relaxation and desensitisation therapy instead.

This technique requires medical dilators, or as an alternative you can use your husbands fingers. Dilators can be prescribed by your sex therapist or family physician. Make sure before you attempt this technique that your husband's fingernails are clean and are clipped short, free of sharp edges. Dilators should be cleaned and brought to body temperature beforehand in warm water.

To start, have your husband part the inner and outer labia, gently exposing the opening of the vagina. He should generously lubricate his index finger or the smallest dilator and place it at the entrance of the vagina and stop.

Now gently squeeze the walls of your vagina until you feel them start to fatigue and spontaneously relax, just like you do during your kegels. A strong mind-muscle connection is essential to doing this effectively, so make sure you practice your kegels well beforehand.

Once your muscles start to fatigue, you will feel an involuntary relaxation of the bulbocavernosus muscles at the entrance to your vagina. When you feel the muscles relaxing, let your husband know by giving him a sign or using a code word you both agree on. Then he should advance his index finger or the first dilator about half an inch to an inch into your vagina and then stop. Feel free to tell him to stop sooner than this point if you start to feel some resistance.

Now relax. Concentrate on how this feels. Allow yourself to get used to the sensation. After a few moments, you will feel your vaginal muscles contracting around the dilator or his finger. When you are ready, start squeezing again, aiming to once again fatigue and spontaneously relax the muscles. This time you will be squeezing against the first few inches of your husband's finger or the dilator, so it may feel a little different from when he started. As before, once you feel the muscles fatiguing and your vagina relaxing, ask your husband to advance his finger or the dilator another half inch or so.

You should repeat this procedure until he's able to advance the entire dilator or finger. How does this feel? Concentrate on the parts of your vagina that feel most pleasurable, and encourage him to sweep gently up and down, side to side and round and round. Experiment with very light touch, light touch, firm pressure and deep pressure. Which ones give you the most pleasure? Let him know what these are, and explore the feeling of sexual satisfaction they give you.

At this point the first dilator or the index finger is fully inserted. For different couples, getting here might take twenty minutes, two hours or the entire night. *There is no need to rush.* Take your time. You have the rest of your lives to enjoy each other.

When you have gotten used to the sensation of the first dilator or one finger, your husband should pull it out slowly and gently, then start the process all over again with the second dilator or two fingers. Using the same technique, make sure that you both are adjusting the speed and depth of penetration to your comfort, stopping when there is discomfort and using lots and lots of lubrication. Ensure that you've fatigued the muscles completely before advancing, as this is key to preventing pain.

Continue this process in order of increasing dilator size or using one, two and three fingers in succession. This gradual process is essential to gently widening the hymen rather than tearing it, as well as fully relaxing the vagina. It takes longer, but it is much less painful than attempting to burst it open all at once. When your husband is able to fully insert the largest dilator or three fingers, then your hymen should be stretched enough for penile insertion.

Introducing the penis for the first time will follow the same process as the dilators or fingers, but this time, your husband should place his generously lubricated penis at the entrance of your vagina and advance when you give the cue. Squeeze gently as you did before, and once you feel your vagina fatiguing, give the signal for him to advance. He should go in only about half an inch at a time, with you repeating the squeezing and relaxing each time. Continue squeezing and advancing until the entire length of his penis is inside you. If your husband's penis is on the larger side, keep going until you can't take any more. It might be a little painful for your husband when you squeeze, so please be gentle if he starts to yelp!

Don't be in a hurry to thrust. Your vagina still needs to get used to your husband's penis. Again, experiment with very light touch, light touch, firm pressure and deep pressure. Feel free to add more lube as required.

Once you feel ready, your husband can start thrusting gently, picking up the pace when it feels right to. Now you can match his motion with yours and enjoy the rhythmical oscillation of both your hips as they dance in synchrony, uniting your bodies, souls and spirits together, giving glory to God!

Congratulations, you have just made love for the first time!

A growing number of newly-weds are choosing to delay making love for the first time, until the day after (or even a few days after) the wedding. It makes perfect sense too; some weddings, especially African and Asian ceremonies, can hold over the entire weekend, and even shorter events can involve several dress changes and many activities. Most couples don't get into their hotel room until evening or even after midnight. If this is you, then it's perfectly fine if you and your husband don't feel up to rolling in the sheets just yet. Take your time! You both have the rest of your lives together, so there is no rush.

If you are anything like the couple in the Songs of Songs, you won't be able to delay having sex for too long after your wedding. If you or your husband are comfortable going weeks without consummating your marriage then there are likely to be some serious underlying concerns that need urgent attention. Please speak to a trusted counsellor, pastor or sex therapist as soon as you can.

Aftercare

You might feel a bit sore for some time after your first sex, and if you bled, it may take a few moments to stop completely.

There will be some bodily fluids to clean up afterwards as well, so keep some wet wipes and paper towels close by. One of our clients, a lady called Chiamaka, told us how she was not prepared for the mess created by all the fluids that seemed to 'pour out from everywhere' after she and her husband had sex for the first time. She quickly realised that she could not bear the thought of semen, vaginal fluids and sweat soiling her precious sheets.

We advised her to keep several large towels or blankets by their bed in an easy-to-reach cabinet so that she could protect the linen each time they made love. These were then washed and replaced regularly after use. If you and your husband are more adventurous, you can have a few sex blankets scattered around the house in places you are more likely to have sex, like the kitchen, living room or stairs—even in the car—so that you are always prepared.

Another client, Efua, insisted on having a shower immediately after sex. It turned out she had heard somewhere about a ritual ablution that was necessary to wash away the impurities of sex after lovemaking.

We had to help Efua understand that the requirements of the law in Leviticus 15:18 are no longer binding on believers who partake of the divine nature (2 Peter 1:3–4). The old covenant of the law has been superseded by the new covenant in Christ's blood (Hebrews 8:6), and the requirements of the levitical law have been fulfilled in the death of the sinless Lamb (Romans 10:4). Taking a bath right after sex should be seen more as a matter of personal preference, and not one of adherence to the law.

Personally however, we feel that rushing off immediately can rob you of the opportunity to cuddle and bond with your husband after sex. Here is a secret: some of the most intimate, authentic and vulnerable conversations you can have with your husband happen when you are wrapped in his embrace just after you have made love! So don't rush away too soon after sex is over; enjoy the bliss of lying in each other's arms, and make it a habit to talk to each other afterward. Here is another secret: most men fall asleep soon after anyway, so you can sneak off and shower when he nods off! However, if you can't bear the thought of stewing in both your bodily fluids, then by all means, do what feels best for you.

We believe wholeheartedly that your first sexual encounter can be a beautiful and memorable experience, but it requires planning, preparation and intentionality.

Do you think you could try the Craig Technique? If you do, we would love to hear from you.

Prayer

Dear Lord, thank You for the beauty of sex in marriage. Thank You because now I know that You were not excluding me from it—You were reserving it for me. In Jesus's name, amen!

9
Practical Sex Tips

The first time you have sex might be a little awkward. There is the whole other person on top of and inside you, and you are probably feeling sensations that you have never felt before.

There are some practical things that you will want to take care of beforehand, because midway through lovemaking may not be the best time to pause and make arrangements for something you could have sorted well ahead of time.

We had no clue about some of these practical matters because no one told us. We found out the hard way. Perhaps you don't have to.

Starter Pack

Pregame

If it's your first time, you want to feel as beautiful and as confident as you can. Get a manicure and pedicure the day before, and throw in a massage if you can. It can also be helpful to have a mini pamper session just before you get in bed. Throw on some special lingerie to enhance the experience for both of you. A shower or a bath soak, your favourite moisturiser or hand cream—do what works for you.

Pray

Say a prayer as husband and wife just before you get busy. Nothing long and fancy—just tell God how you feel and how blessed it is to finally be able to experience the gift of marriage. Don't worry if your 'amens' are swallowed by his kisses. It's all part of the plan.

Relaxation

We all hold a lot of unconscious tension in our bodies, and sometimes this can get in the way of us experiencing pleasure during sex. Endeavor to make your sex session as relaxing as possible. Remember to take deep breaths, let your muscles relax fully and maximise the intensity of every sensation.

Lubrication

Lube is your friend. We can't say this enough. The more, the better. Remember that the amount of natural vaginal wetness a woman produces bears no correlation to how aroused she is or how much desire she has for her husband. Some women produce a lot of natural lubrication, and some others not so much. If you are planning on getting pregnant right away (more on this later), then oil-based lubricants are fine, but if you are using condoms, then water-based lubricants are best. Don't forget about the fan. Point it away!

Hydration

Sex is thirsty business, so keep a bottle of water by your bedside for hydration, preferably one with a straw or spout that you can sip from without spilling the water. Remember to take water breaks in between lovemaking sessions to keep your love engines going.

Pillows

One of the best ways to improve the depth of penetration and the intensity of your pleasure is to position your pelvis to allow for different angles of penetration. To do this, prop a pillow under your hips and back to angle your vagina in a 30- to 45-degree tilt towards the ceiling.

Dance

Try to match your husband's rhythm and tempo. This way not only are you an active participant in lovemaking, but you can control the depth and speed of penetration as well. One method is to meet his thrusts halfway by moving your hips up to meet his. (Expect some smacking sounds.) Alternatively, you can move your hips in the opposite direction to allow for extra-long strokes. Careful not to move too far in the opposite direction so his penis does not slip out. (Never mind if it does; just slip it back in.)

Farts

Queefing is the slang term for vaginal farts, a normal bodily function that happens when small pockets of air get trapped in the vagina due to the in-and-out thrusting during sex. It is perfectly normal, very common and nothing to be ashamed of. In fact, some people find it to be a turn-on. So fart away!

Secretions

During sex, you might notice some fluid from your Bartholin's gland, a pea-sized structure at your vaginal opening. It and other paravaginal ('around the vagina') glands secrete fluids that add to your natural lubrication during sex. The back-and-forth motion can churn this fluid and turn it creamy or frothy, so don't worry, that's not a yeast infection (unless of course you know you have one).

Burning Pee

Sometimes a woman can develop a urinary tract infection (UTI) after sex, which is characterised by burning pee. This is hilariously called honeymoon cystitis and is actually very common. One of our clients reached out to us crying because she thought her husband had given her an STD (sexually transmitted disease). After we asked a few questions about her symptoms, it turned out that it was just a UTI.

Honeymoon cystitis develops when bacteria on the skin and around the rectum are carried by the penis to the urethra (where you pee from) during sex. These eventually make their way into the bladder to cause infection. If you develop honeymoon cystitis, please consult with your doctor, who will prescribe some treatment for you.

Communication

Tell eachother what feels good during and after sex. Use verbal and non verbal cues. Create your own slang words, safe words and stop words for different sexual activities. Be open and honest about what you want and about how you feel. Sexual satisfaction should be mutual, and both you and your husband should develop the freedom to be authentic with each other, to be able to express your thoughts, desires, expectations and vulnerabilities to one another.

Positions

There are probably over a thousand sex positions, ranging from relatively easy to extremely difficult. Some of the more difficult positions have very little utility outside confirming that a couple have the gymnastic and acrobatic prowess to pull them off. Don't worry—we won't be including any of those here. We want to give you a few simple and straightforward starter positions to get you off to a good start.[1] As your sexual experience deepens, you will discover new and more exciting positions that you can add to your repertoire.

We teach that sex has three primary purposes:

1. Pregnancy

2. Pleasure

3. Intimacy

Whatever your goal or goals, there is a sexual position that is just right for you.

To keep things simple, we will lay out our suggested starter positions into these three categories. To be clear, every one of these positions has the potential to get you pregnant, bring you pleasure and create intimacy with you and your husband. What we hope to achieve by this classification is to show which positions are best at doing what.

Positions for Getting Pregnant

Any position that ensures your husband's sperm successfully makes the journey from your vagina into your uterus is thought to be best for pregnancy. Typically, this requires deep penetration on your husband's part and a tilted pelvis on yours. Scientific studies examining the basis of this theory are open to interpretation, but we think it's a good idea for what it's worth.

Front entry, man on top, woman spreadeagle, knees bent:

Lie on your back facing up, and support your lower back and hips with a conventional pillow or a dedicated sex pillow. Spread your legs wide, then bend your knees toward your stomach to form a cradle.

Your husband can now penetrate your vagina from the front and support his weight by leaning into the cradle and holding your knees.

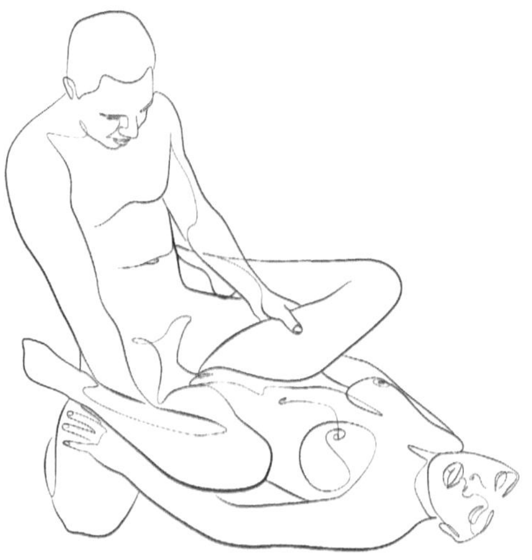

Front entry, man on top, woman's ankles on man's shoulders:

Lie on your back facing up. Raise both legs up, feet pointing towards the ceiling or the sky. Gently place your ankles on his shoulders (have your husband kneel in front of you if you need help getting them up there). He penetrates your vagina from the front by lifting your hips to align with his, and he supports the weight of your legs on his shoulders. You can alternate the position by crossing your legs or by bending your knees and putting your feet on his chest.

Rear entry, man on top, woman lying on front:

Lie face down with a firm angled support underneath your hips. Your husband lies on top of you and penetrates your vagina from behind. He can support himself either on his hands or on his elbows to vary the height of approach. Change the opening between your legs to vary the depth of penetration.

Positions for Female Pleasure

Only the first few inches of the vagina have pleasure-producing nerve endings, but there are a wide range of pleasure sensations in the deeper parts of the vagina which are thought to come from indirect stimulation of the clitoral complex just beneath the labia. Some of the best positions for female pleasure include those that allow the woman to control the depth, angle and speed of penetration.

Front entry, woman on top, face to face, man lying face up:

Have your husband lie on his back facing up. Straddle his hips, aligning your vagina just over his erect penis. You can choose to plant your feet firmly on the surface or bend your knees so that you are kneeling. Slowly lower your hips onto his, using your hands on his chest or legs as support. Use your hands and legs to vary the depth of penetration. Switch things up by turning around to face his feet, to give him full view of your derrière.

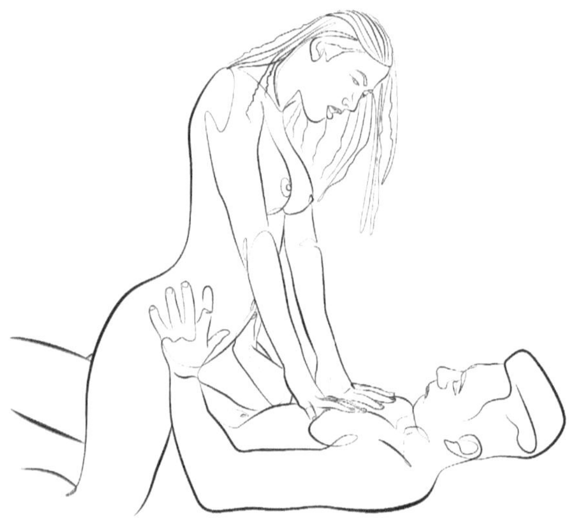

Front approach, clitoral stimulation, woman lying face up:

Lie on the edge of the bed facing up. Spread your legs wide and bend your knees. Your husband can now approach from the front to stimulate your clitoris with his fingers, his kisses or both, depending on your preference. You can support your feet at the edge of the bed or place them on your husband's shoulders.

Rear entry, woman on all fours:

Start from a kneeling position, and then go onto all fours by bending over and supporting your upper body with your hands on the bed. Your husband then kneels behind you on the bed, or stands on the floor, and penetrates your vagina from behind by aligning your hips with his. You can choose to have him kneel or stand in between your open legs or have your closed legs slotted through his. Vary the depth of penetration by moving your weight from your hands to your elbows and if possible, to your chest as shown in the diagram.

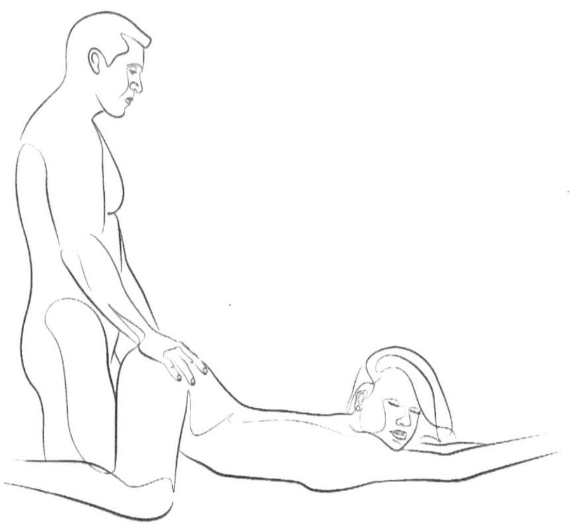

Positions for Intimacy

Some of the most intimate positions are those where you and your husband's bodies have as much contact as possible, not just your hips. This way you both are able to feel as close to the other as possible while still enjoying the pleasure of love-making.

Rear entry, both lying on sides, woman in front:

Lie on your side with your knees bent towards your chest. Your husband lies behind you and penetrates your vagina from behind, wrapping you in his warm embrace. You both can take turns to bend your knees to vary the depth of penetration and adjust the speed of entry.

Front entry, face to face, man sitting, woman straddling:

Have your husband sit on the bed or a chair. Straddling his hips, align your vagina just over his erect penis. Wrap your hands around his neck and your legs around his waist or plant them firmly on the floor. Using your feet as a fulcrum, vary the depth of penetration by moving your hips in and out, up and down—or for a different sensation, try moving slowly in a gentle circular motion.

Front entry, face to face, man on top:

Lie on your back facing up, and support your lower back and hips with a conventional pillow or a sex pillow. Spread your legs wide, then your husband lies on top of you and penetrates your vagina from the front, supporting his weight on his hands or elbows. You can now enjoy deep kisses or intimate whispers while looking into his eyes.

Orgasms

Sexual pleasure is built up and stored in the nervous system, like water behind a dam filling up a reservoir. During foreplay and throughout sex, every pleasurable stimulation adds some water to the orgasm reservoir. When the water rises past a set threshold (this is different for every woman), then the built-up tension crashes through the dam and is released in waves of pleasure and involuntary rhythmic contractions of the pelvic muscles and the rest of the body. This release of built-up sexual pleasure is an orgasm.

We mentioned before that we believe most women can orgasm. Most men do, so why not women? The penis and the clitoris develop in our mothers' wombs from the exact same embryonic tissue, and only become different structures by the seventh week of pregnancy in response to either oestrogen or testosterone (which is determined by the genetic sex of the foetus). This is where their similarities end.

The male penis serves several functions:

1. It hardens to penetrate the vagina for sex

2. It is an organ of pleasure during sex

3. It is the passageway for sperm to exit the male and fertilise the egg

4. It is the channel for urine to pass outside the body

The clitoris has only one function: it was made to experience pleasure!

Even though penises and vaginas are made of similar tissues, they are shaped differently and are organised differently. Each organ will require a different kind of stimulation to produce the most pleasurable response.

The Clitoris has
only one function: it
was made to experience
Pleasure!

We conducted an online survey which showed that 95 per cent of men said that they have an orgasm every time they have penetrative intercourse. For women, having an orgasm from intercourse is much less guaranteed. In a 2015 study of over 10,000 participants, 46 per cent of women said that they always or nearly always had an orgasm when having intercourse, with only 6 per cent of women reporting always having an orgasm.[2] Could you imagine how differently our world would view sex if the vast majority of men never had an orgasm when they had sex?

We have a theory about the orgasm divide: Could it have something to do with the particular techniques used when people have sex? Is it possible that the most popular forms of sexual contact have focused on the techniques that maximise male pleasure and neglected those that emphasise female pleasure?

Let's explain what we mean. The most sensitive part of the penis is the *frenulum*, and this little lip under the head of the penis gets the most stimulation from back-and-forth motion. Oral sex, handjobs and the overwhelming majority of sex positions are set up in a way that maximise the opportunity for back-and-forth stimulation of the penis. Little wonder that almost all men will reach orgasm within a few minutes of penetrative sexual intercourse.

The clitoris, on the other hand, is a complex organ, and science has only just recently mapped its full extent with functional magnetic resonance imaging (fMRI) techniques. The most sensitive part of the clitoris is yet to be agreed on, but we can assume that the tip of the clitoris, the G-spot and the anterior fornix erogenous zone (AFE, or A-spot) are in close competition for first place.

The tip of the clitoris responds best to rhythmical flicks, gentle suction or rotational motion. The G-spot responds to sustained curved flicking or direct tapping, while the A-spot (located deep in the vagina) responds best to deep upward sloping pressure. Back-and-forth motion can only stimulate these areas indirectly, and does not even come close to the direct methods of stimulation that are listed here.

No wonder most women never reach orgasm. Back-and-forth, in-and-out sex just does not cut it. Sadly, the sexual repertoire of most couples is extremely limited and does not incorporate the techniques that are guaranteed to maximise female pleasure and culminate in her reaching orgasm.

As we said before, when a woman experiences pleasure during penetration, most of that sensation is coming from indirect stimulation of the clitoris. In fact, Michael Castleman in his article 'The Woman's Erotic Zone' claims that the vagina is not the primary sex organ for women. The clitoris, he says, is a woman's primary sex organ.[3] We could not agree more.

He writes:

> Actually, the vagina is a sex organ for men. They slide in their erections and ejaculate there. Men love the vagina. It provides such pleasure. But for women, the vagina is not much of a sex organ. It's a *reproductive* organ. At term, babies surf through it into the world. Most women derive most of their erotic pleasure not from vaginal fingering or intercourse, but from gentle caressing of the Clitoral System: the little nub, the inner lips, the outer urethral sponge, and the inner sponge/G-spot.

We believe that almost all women can experience orgasm if they and their husbands explore the full range of touch and use stimulation techniques that are specific for producing maximum female sexual response.

Now, having said that, if your husband is doing all the right moves and you still have trouble reaching orgasm, it might be that you have a very sensitive SIS and a relatively insensitive SES. Perhaps it takes a lot of stimulation to activate your SES enough to generate the level of sexual tension required to fill your orgasm reservoir, and it takes only a little bit of anxiety or stress for your body to hit the brakes.

The good news is that because your SIS is developed in response to your experiences, belief systems and upbringing, it can be altered and modified. There is evidence to suggest that women who initially started off with an overactive SIS have gone on to rewire that aspect of their subconscious using affirmation techniques, but most importantly with a loving, patient and gentle partner who helps them overcome their inhibitions and fears.

However, when all is said and done, you must remember that the goal of sex is not orgasm. Ask the couple who are timing their lovemaking so that they can conceive and have a child after ten years of marriage. Or the couple who are making love on their sixty-fifth wedding anniversary. Or even the woman who pleases her husband using her kisses or her hands knowing that her actions will not bring her any direct pleasure in return. None of these scenarios focuses on orgasm. It should not matter how many times or how powerfully you climax. What matters more is the intimacy that sex creates and the pleasure you bring each other.

Society focuses on masculine pleasure at the expense of the woman from whom the man derives it. We believe that this is not God's original plan. If a woman can orgasm, then she should. We encourage you to make room within your sexual repertoire for activities that bring you pleasure. Communicate honestly and openly to let your husband know what works for you. **Take responsibility for your pleasure** by using positions and techniques that maximise your pleasure while at the same time giving him pleasure and creating intimacy. Keep a mental map of your own buttons and levers, and revisit this list often to refine it by adding new discoveries and recycling old tricks that you may have forgotten.

One of the ways to discover new things is through regular exploratory sex.

Exploratory Sex

Whenever clients come to us complaining that the spark has died in their sex lives, we always give them the exploratory sex homework, and the results have mostly been positive. If you and your husband incorporate exploratory sex into your sex routines, it could very well mean that you never linger too long in the dry patches that most couples often visit.

Each partner takes turns to have an exploratory sex day, and during sex that day the goal is to explore every erogenous zone from top to bottom, using the results to create a personalised pleasure map for each of you. Experiment with different intensities of touch, stretch, cold, heat and vibration (just like we discussed in Chapter 4) to determine what areas respond best to what kind of touch or stimulation, then draw a new sexual map of dos and don'ts, dislikes, likes and must-haves.

In addition to the erogenous zones we listed previously, once you are married, you can explore the following as well:

Sexual Erogenous Zones

1. Breasts
2. Mons pubis
3. Vagina
4. Clitoris

5. Anterior fornix

6. G-spot

7. Prepuce

8. Fourchette .

We explore this and in more detail in the HIGMT workbook which is available on our website.

Contraception

We are advocates for family spacing, and one way to do this is by using contraception. Almost all churches (other than the Catholic Church) agree that contraception as a means to space a family is permitted. All churches agree that using contraception to promote promiscuity is wrong. This is our position as well. Please speak with your pastor or priest if you feel unsure about using contraception due to your convictions, so you can receive guidance and advice specific to your circumstances.

When we started out in ministry, we used to advise that couples wait at least a year to have children so they could get to know each other better as husband and wife and iron out any kinks before bringing a child into the mix. Even though this advice might seem wise on the surface, we now know that it is not always practical or desirable for every couple. For example, some of our clients who are mature singles are keen to get pregnant right away.

We have seen couples get pregnant on the wedding night and go on to sail through their first years of marriage without much turbulence, while others have waited a year or two only to face difficult and seemingly insurmountable challenges when their first baby was born.

This is what we now advise: however long you choose to wait, make sure you enjoy each other's company first. Get to know each other. Plan ahead for your children, and then prayerfully bring them forth.

If you do decide to space your children, we think it is very important that you speak with your husband and agree with him on how long you both want to wait, as this will influence what kind of contraception you can use.

If you want to wait a month or two, then condoms may be a good idea. There are many brands that mimic a natural feel and extend the pleasure for both partners. Some even have textures to enhance the female's pleasure.

If you are looking at a year to three years, then the implant or the pill might be a good idea. These are subject to your medical history, and you will need to discuss this with a suitably trained doctor or your obstetrician and gynaecologist.

If you want to wait three to five years or longer, then you might want to consider a long-acting reversible contraceptive like the implant or the coil. Again, please speak to your family physician or ob-gyn so they can provide you with a detailed and personalised recommendation based on your specific circumstances and medical history.

Gourmet Sex vs Fast-Food Sex

Some nights you and your husband might make love for hours and hours, while some days it might be all over in less than three minutes flat. Don't be dismayed. There is a place for fast food and a place for five-course meals. It is healthy and balanced to have a bit of both.

We try to have date night every two weeks, and sometimes it can be as simple as ordering a pizza and snuggling in front of the television for a good movie. Some other nights we make it a big deal and dress up in our best clothes, reserve a table at a fancy restaurant and order exotic dishes in languages we don't understand. Cue the duck confit, filet mignon and creme brulee.

We wouldn't have pizza every night. It's just not healthy. But we wouldn't advise fine dining every night either; it would lose its special appeal (and cost a fortune!). You see how this balance keeps things interesting and healthy. We believe the same is true for sex. There have been times when we have made love all through the weekend, experiencing waves and waves of pleasure, and enjoying deeper and deeper intimacy, but there have also been times when sex is a hurried quickie just before work or sleepy spooning just before bed. We have come to treasure both. You should too!

Prayer:

Dear Lord, thank You for the joys of sex and the way You have orchestrated the human body to fit so perfectly one into the other. I commit my sex life with my husband into Your hands. Help all that we do, bring honour and glory to You. In Jesus's name, amen!

Notes

1. *Christian sex positions?*: Certain indigenous tribes living along the Bight of Bonny in West Africa, especially the Efik-Ibibio language groups, are known to have had a rich traditional history of marriage preparation. In their culture, young maidens were prepared for marriage by the mothers and grandmothers of the village in what was known as the 'fattening room'. This involved months of seclusion and pampering, where the maidens were given daily traditional spa treatments, fed the most delectable meals and taught everything about how to be a wife.

Part of the curriculum during their six months of isolation might have included some of the things we are teaching here in this chapter. When the European missionaries arrived, almost all traditional and cultural practices, regardless of utility, were lumped together as idolatrous and discarded by those who converted to Christianity.

There is an apocryphal story, made popular by Alfred Kinsey, about how the missionary style came to be known by that name. Purportedly it was the European missionaries' preferred sexual position, which they taught as the exclusive way to have sex that was pleasing to God. They supposedly viewed the other sexual positions performed by the indigenous tribes as primitive and barbaric.

We know now that neither of these assumptions is true. There are no good or bad sex positions in marriage. The angle of entry during penetration or the spatial orientation of a couple's body during penovaginal intercourse has no moral value in and of itself, and there is no inherent virtue in practicing one style over another.

2. Kontula O, Anneli M, 'Determinants of Female Sexual Orgasms', *Socioaffective Neuroscience & Psychology*, 6/1 (25 Oct. 2016), doi:10.3402/snp.v6.31624

3. Castleman, Michael, 'The Woman's Erotic Zone', *Psychology Today*, https://www.psychologytoday.com/gb/blog/all-about-sex/201605/the-womans-erotic-zone, accessed 10 Jul. 2021.

10
Sex Is Worship

Something deeply spiritual and immensely powerful happens when a man and his wife have sex. Each time a couple come together, scripture affirms that they become one flesh, and we believe that great potential for spiritual power is made available in an act that can take two separate entities and meld them into one.

> Don't you realize that your bodies are actually parts of Christ? Should a man take his body, which is part of Christ, and join it to a prostitute? Never! And don't you realize that if a man joins himself to a prostitute, he becomes one body with her? For the Scriptures say, 'The two are united into one.' But the person who is joined to the Lord is one spirit with him.
>
> 1 Corinthians 6: 15–17

God designed that when we have sex, our bodies, our souls and our spirits unite. We become *one* with the other person in complete and total union. This union of bodies, souls and spirits is profoundly important, because although the vowing to become husband and wife happens at the altar in the church, the actual becoming *'one flesh'* (Mark 10:7–8) happens on the altar in the bedroom.

In that awesome moment of complete oneness, two bodies join, two souls swirl and two spirits combine! When the dance is over, our bodies may release their embrace, and our spirits may gently untwine, but our souls? They stay connected! There remains a lasting connection between your soul and the soul of every person you have sex with. Little imprints of who they are stay with you, and you literally carry them around with you wherever you go.

We believe that sex was designed by God to be a powerful transcendental event, where a husband and his wife can in that moment feel what it was like to be one in union as they were before Eve was taken from Adam's side. When a husband and wife make love, they re-enact the time when creation was new, when all humanity was in the loins of our progenitors, and we had direct access to the Father.

But that's not all. When a married couple have sex, God for the briefest of moments allows them to experience the inexplicable, how it must feel to be triune. That feeling of being a separate entity but at the same time being one with another; distinct beings, yet part of a larger whole. At the height of sexual passion, whose name do most people call out? That's right—*God*! Is that a coincidence? We don't think so. In that moment, heaven and earth unite again, and our lips involuntarily call out His name.

When you have sex, you unite all three parts of your being with another person—first your body, then your soul and then your spirit; the six strands of both your beings, wrapped up together in harmonious ecstasy. But guess what? If a couple are believers, and they make their union a deliberate act of worship, then the triune God joins them right there in the mix—Father, Son and Holy Spirit, inhabiting the praises of His people! This ninefold cord? Unbreakable!

And so God is inextricably part of the sex act. He is not embarrassed by our pleasure, no! He delights in it! It brings Him joy.

When you have sex with your husband, we invite you to see lovemaking through the lens of worship. Every sound you make can be a 'praise the Lord', every move you make can be a 'hallelujah'. When you think this way, you recognise the significance of the lifelong covenant we make when we say our vows. Priests are usually sworn to their deity for the rest of their lives; similarly, you and your husband set up an altar when you have sex for the first time and consecrate yourselves as lifelong priests upon that altar in service of the Lord.

Have you ever noticed how almost all ancient pagan religions had some form of sex ritual incorporated into their worship practice? Their temples had prostitutes and maidens dedicated to their gods and goddesses, offering worshippers deeper access to the divine through the portal of sex. Eastern mystics and tantric gurus offer sexual experiences with deep esoteric significance as a way to unite with the singularity. African idol worship has rituals that involve sex with designated persons as a means of power or wealth transfer.

This is not a coincidence! The devil takes what is originally God's design and corrupts it for his use.

When you make love and worship, you unlock a powerful place of prayer and intercession that we believe is not attainable in any other way. When two believers touch and agree in prayer, the Bible says God harkens to their prayer; how much more, when a man and a wife join together during sex and are united together as one?

We invite you to invoke the power of this altar in your marriage, so that each time you lie together and pray together, you can see God move mightily on your behalf.

Prayer:

We worship You, Lord, right here and right now! Thank You for uncovering the hidden mysteries and revealing them to us. Yes! Yes! Yes!

CONCLUSION: THIS IS JUST THE BEGINNING

Congratulations on taking the first step in your journey to cultivating a healthy and holy sex life with your husband. We hope you have been blessed by reading our book. There is so much more to learn about godly sex and sexuality, and we have barely scratched the surface of this hugely important topic.

We would like to encourage you to only seek out wholesome biblical sources of sex information as you embark on your journey of sexual discovery. It can sometimes seem harder to find than mainstream or secular sources but if you know where to look you will find that the Lord always leves himself a witness

It is our prayer that as you develop the skills and confidence you need in the bedroom, you will continue to explore and improve on these with further study and a lifelong commitment to learning.

While sex is a vital part of any healthy Christian marriage, it is important to reiterate here that it takes more than good sex to have a good marriage. Prayer, fellowship, deepening intimacy, communication, forgiveness, openness, authenticity and an unwavering commitment to your husband arc some of the very many ingredients you will need to make your marriage a success.

We pray that as you start your new lives together, your desire for each other will continue to grow, and that as the seasons of life change, your love for and commitment to each other will be a constant anchor in uncertain seas. May your love last your lifetimes. In Jesus's name, amen.

Prayer

Almighty God! My marriage will be a reflection of Your glory, and through it, many shall come to know You. Because we have built our relationship on You, the Solid Rock, we will have no fear of the storm. In Jesus's name, amen.

SCRIPTURE QUOTATIONS

Scripture quotations noted CEB are from the *Common English Bible Study Bible*. Copyright © 2011 The Common English Bible, Nashville, Tennessee. Used by permission.

Scripture quotations noted CEV are from the *Contemporary English Version*, Copyright © 1991, 1992, 1995 by American Bible Society. Used by permission.

Scripture quotations noted ESV are from the *English Standard Version*, ESV® Bible (The Holy Bible, *English Standard Version®*), copyright © 2001 by Crossway Bibles, a publishing ministry of Good News Publishers. Used by permission. All rights reserved.

Scripture quotations noted GNT are from the *Good News Translation*, © 1994 published by the Bible Societies/HarperCollins Publishers Ltd UK, Good News Bible © American Bible Society 1966, 1971, 1976, 1992. Used with permission.

Scripture quotations noted NASB are from the *New American Standard Bible*. Copyright The Lockman Foundation 1960, 1962, 1963, 1968, 1971, 1972, 1973, 1975, 1977. Used by permission.

Scripture quotations noted NET are from the New Englis Translation, NET Bible® copyright ©1996, 2019 used with permission from Biblical Studies Press, L.L.C. All rights reserved.

Scripture quotations noted NIV are from the *New International Version®*, NIV®. Copyright © 1973, 1978, 1984, 2011 by Biblica, Inc.™ Used by permission of Zondervan. All rights reserved worldwide. The 'NIV' and 'New International Version' are trademarks registered in the United States Patent and Trademark Office by Biblica, Inc.™

ACKNOWLEDGEMENTS

Thank you Abba for your love. Thank you Jesus for your sacrifice. Thank you Holy Spirit for your inspiration. We love you more than words can say.

This book would not have made it off our hearts and into your hands were it not for the love, dedication and professionalism of a lot of amazing people. We would like to thank a few of them:

Thank you Rev. Dr. Yemi Amusan, our mentor, teacher and friend, for being a beacon of inspiration and a wellspring of wisdom.

Thank you Pastor Kingsley and Mildred Okonkwo for your accurate consistency over the past twenty-five years and for graciously writing the foreword to this book.

Thank you to our dear pastors, Pastor Paul and Ifeanyi Adefarasin, senior pastors of House on the Rock International (HOTR); Apostle Goodheart and Pastor Abimbola Ekwueme of Revival House of Glory International Church (RHOGIC); Pastor Uche Aigbe, the resident pastor of House on the Rock Abuja; and Pastor Temi Odejide, the resident pastor of House on the Rock London.

Thank you to our family and friends who acted as sounding boards, many of whom were the first readers of this book in its many stages. Your patience and feedback helped us develop what was once a three-page email into a full-fledged book series: Temilola Craig, Jemima Yusuf, Damilola Ladeinde,

Erinne Mcclean, Oludara Egerton-Shyngle, Fifunmi and Amaka Odunowo, Busayo Adepegba, Tolu Oloruntoba, Joy Ehonwa, Ife Iyaniwura, Nguavese Obemeata, Iberedem Ewang, Yeside Agboola and Arit Okpo.

Thank you Saadiya Oniwon, Joycelyn Esangbedo, Victoria Ogunrombi and Munachi Osisiogu for giving our vision clarity.

Thank you Christina Roth for your expertise and friendship. Your steady hand took our shaky ones and gently showed us that we too have what it takes to weave a beautiful tapestry of words. Thank you El Mehdi Najdi for accurately and faithfully translating our vision into tasteful illustrations.

Finally, we wish to thank all the couples we counselled who have given us permission to share their personal stories. To protect their privacy, we have changed their names and blended their stories so that they cannot be identified.

THANK YOU GIFT

We hope and pray that this book has been a blessing to you.

As a thank you, We would love to share with you the companion online workbook and prayer guide that we have specially prepared for this book. In it you will find step by step instructional guides and tools to deepen your knowledge and understanding of the concepts discussed here.

Please visit higmt.olamidecraig.com/gift to get your free copy today.

ABOUT THE AUTHORS

Olamide and Aisha are Jesus lovers.

David Olamide Craig is a pastor, doctor and sex educator. He has a master's in Occupational Health from the University of Birmingham and is a member of the Royal College of General Practitioners in the United Kingdom. In 2001 he started the Dianoia Foundation in the University of Ibadan, a ministry dedicated to teaching sexual purity.

Aisha Nkiru Craig works in finance as a business analyst. She is a member of the Chartered Governance Institute UK and Ireland. She is a beauty entrepreneur and an avid explorer of exotic places and experimental cuisine. She grew up in church, and her father was the resident pastor of the Gospel Pentecostal Assembly in Lagos. She went on to work full time at the House on the Rock Church, Abuja, where she met her husband, Dr. Craig.

Aisha and Olamide live with their daughter, Chidinma, in a Scandinavian eco-home overlooking a tranquil brook that babbles through a lush Buckinghamshire meadow. Together they have over twenty-five years of experience in church ministry and relationship counselling.

Through their non-profit, the Craig Christian Center, they offer pre-engagement counselling, premarital counselling, wedding night prep classes and sex therapy sessions for young couples. They are authors of The Good*Christian Sex Guide series.

ABOUT THE GOOD*CHRISTIAN SEX GUIDE

The Bible never tells us that sex is sinful, or evil, or wrong. Instead of preaching that sex equals sin, the church should be teaching believers that **sex is righteous but reserved.** Reserved for a *specific person* (husband and wife) and for a *specific time* (after marriage).

Sadly, the church has shied away from a biblically holistic view of sex education, and instead focuses on teaching abstinence only, neglecting to provide the robust framework without which abstinence cannot survive.

While we wholeheartedly believe in saving sex for marriage, we are all too aware that 'virginity-focused' abstinence-only teaching has proved unsuccessful in preventing sex before marriage.

This lack of well-rounded, biblical sexuality teaching also means that believers are filling the vacuum with information from secular and often sinful sources. Learning about sex from locker rooms, music videos, movies or porn creates unrealistic expectations of sex and envelops it in shame and taboo.

In a world where young children are being exposed to online pornography, the result is a measurable increase in underage sexual activity, teenage pregnancy, sexually transmitted diseases and abortion.

Our mission is to change the way Christians learn about sex. This book and the others in this series provide a no-holds-barred, full-on, faith-based perspective on sex and sexuality and will serve as a trusted authoritative source of sexuality information that Christians can reference for guidance and instruction.

It is our hope that as we return to the full biblical teaching on sex, we can raise a generation of sex-positive Christians who not only honour God with their sexuality, but are well-equipped to navigate their increasingly sexualised world without conforming to it.

For more information on who we are and what we do, please visit us at www.olamidecraig.com.

NOTES AND REFLECTIONS

www.ingramcontent.com/pod-product-compliance
Lightning Source LLC
Chambersburg PA
CBHW032252070726
47590CB00016B/2495